# PARACORD PROJECTS
## FOR CAMPING AND OUTDOOR SURVIVAL

# PARACORD PROJECTS
## FOR CAMPING AND OUTDOOR SURVIVAL

### PRACTICAL AND ESSENTIAL USES FOR THE ULTIMATE TOOL IN YOUR PACK

BRYAN LYNCH
author of *Victorinox Swiss Army Knife
Camping & Outdoor Survival Guide*

FOX CHAPEL
PUBLISHING

**Note: While paracord is an extremely strong and versatile material, it should never be substituted for proper climbing rope and gear.**

ISBN 978-1-4971-0045-9

Library of Congress Control Number: 2019024142

To learn more about the other great books from Fox Chapel Publishing, or to find a retailer near you, call toll-free
800-457-9112 or visit us at *www.FoxChapelPublishing.com.*

We are always looking for talented authors. To submit an idea, please send a brief inquiry to acquisitions@foxchapelpublishing.com.

Printed in Singapore
First printing

Because working with paracord and other materials inherently includes the risk of injury and damage, this book cannot guarantee that creating the projects in this book is safe for everyone. For this reason, this book is sold without warranties or guarantees of any kind, expressed or implied, and the publisher and the author disclaim any liability for any injuries, losses, or damages caused in any way by the content of this book or the reader's use of the tools needed to complete the projects presented here. The publisher and the author urge all readers to thoroughly review each project and to understand the use of all tools before beginning any project.

Illustrations by the author.
Photographs other than those listed on page 248 taken by the author.
Some of the paracord and hardware used in this book were provided by Pepperell Braiding Company.

*To my stunning wife, Nikki.*

# CONTENTS

# PREFACE

Although I grew up hunting, fishing, and camping, it was only about fifteen years ago when I first started learning about the wonders of paracord and its many outdoor applications. Paracord is extremely versatile, easy to work with, and affordable. It comes in almost any color or pattern design you could want. I used it to make bracelets, lanyards, dog leashes, dog collars, monkey fists, water bottle holders, slings, belts—the list goes on. At one point, I was making so many things out of paracord that I had almost 20,000 feet (more than 6,000 meters) of it stored in my basement. That's when I decided I had made enough projects for myself!

In the following chapters, I discuss how to use paracord in two ways. First, I give a walkthrough of how to make functional items at home that can be taken into the field and broken down and used in a survival situation. Second, I show you how to use paracord in survival situations (such as making shelters, tools, and so forth).

As Benjamin Franklin wrote, "By failing to prepare, you are preparing to fail." Survival situations can come upon us before we even realize what has happened. In such times, nature doesn't follow our plans. Obviously, one can survive without paracord, but having it with you can be invaluable.

My hope in writing this book is that the projects, tips, and my own experimentation will better acquaint you with paracord and how you can utilize it to its full potential when everything is falling apart.

Paracord is useful and—dare I say it?—fashionable.

# INTRODUCTION

Allied troops parachuting into the Netherlands in 1944.

## The History of Paracord

To understand why paracord is so useful, we should know a little history behind this amazing cordage product. In 1935, American chemist Wallace Carothers (1896–1937), working for DuPont, created a new synthetic material that came to be called nylon. At that time, parachutes were primarily made from silk. However, silk was in short supply because it relies on the silkworm to make it—a slow method of production. Since nylon was quicker to produce, and stronger, it replaced silk in parachutes. Nylon was also used to make the suspension lines—parachute cord, aka *paracord*—for the parachutes. When World War II paratroopers landed on the ground, they would cut the cordage from their chutes and use it to make straps and tie up gear.

### Perfect Paracord!

Did you know that paracord is awesome adventure material?

- It's mildew resistant.

- It shrinks only a little when wet.

- Just about the only thing that will degrade it over time is ultraviolet light.

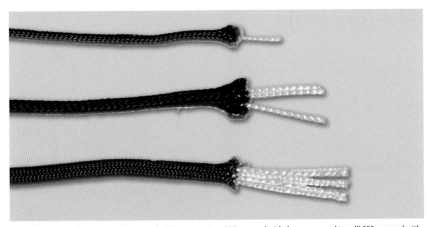

Pictured from top to bottom: type 95 paracord with one yarn, type 325 paracord with three yarns, and type III 550 paracord with seven yarns.

Although it was (and to some extent, still is) primarily a military product, paracord has many civilian uses today. It is especially popular with outdoorspeople, emergency responders, and crafters. It has become so popular, and even trendy, that you've probably seen people wearing paracord bracelets and other accessories as part of their daily wardrobe.

There are several different types of paracord but the most common is type III, often referred to as 550 cord. One piece of cordage can hold 550 pounds (250 kilograms) of static weight. (But don't grab your 550 cord and head for the nearest mountain! Paracord should not be substituted for an actual climbing rope.)

It is important to know the difference between knockoff paracord and real paracord—especially if your life is on the line (pun intended!). Read on to find out how.

There are three bracelet projects in this book—see page 68 when you're ready to make one.

# The Anatomy of Paracord

To properly identify real paracord, we need to break it down into its parts. First, there is the outer woven sheath. Then there is the inner core of strands that are called "yarns." The most common type of paracord, type III 550, has 7–9 yarns. Don't get confused if you hear people talking about paracord and using the word "strands," or "inner strands"—they are referring to the yarns. The yarns, then, are made up of even finer threads of nylon. These can be pulled apart into thinner and thinner pieces depending on what they are needed for.

This structure is what gives paracord its amazing strength relative to its size and weight. It also gives you much more cordage than you think you have, if you are willing to pull the yarns out of the sheath and tie them together end to end.

To get an estimate of how much total yarn cordage you have, add the number of yarns you have plus one (for the outer sheath). Take that number and multiply it by the original length of the paracord. For example, type III paracord generally has seven yarns surrounded by the outer sheath. Add those two numbers together and you get eight. If I have 1 ft. (30 cm) of cordage, I multiply eight times one. That gives me approximately 8 ft. (2.4 m) of total cordage when the paracord is pulled apart. Obviously that number increases

as you increase the original length of intact paracord. A 10 ft. (3 m) piece would produce almost 80 ft. (24 m) of usable cordage! Of course, always keep in mind that some length will be lost to the knots that join the lengths of yardage together.

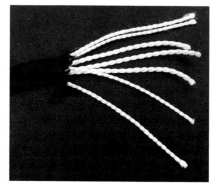

Type III 550 paracord with seven inner yarns.

I cut approximately 1 ft. (30 cm) of type III paracord and laid out the strands below the outer core. If you tie all these ends together, you will have close to 8 ft. (2.4 m) of cordage. Note: Some length is lost in the knots joining the yarns together.

# True Paracord

Not all paracord is created equal. The kind of paracord that you want, and what is used in this book, is "mil-spec," which means that it meets military specifications. Both the yarns and the outer sheath must be made of 100% nylon.

Some knockoff paracord is manufactured with a nylon sheath and inner strands made of polyester. Most people can't tell the difference between polyester and nylon just by looking at them. Here is a quick test you can do to find out what you're looking at. (But don't do this in the store before purchasing it!)

All you need is a cutting tool and a lighter. When two pieces of nylon are melted and pushed together, they will stick to one another like glue. When a piece of nylon and a piece of polyester are melted and pushed together, they will not stick together. So, if you are unsure about the materials in your paracord, try this test. Never risk your life by using sub-par materials.

## PARA-TIP: Check for Strength

If you are reusing paracord, it's a good idea to check its integrity first. Simply pull it through your hands and check the nylon sheath for any nicks or fraying. If you find a damaged section, cut it out or use the cord for a light-duty task.

# PREPPING

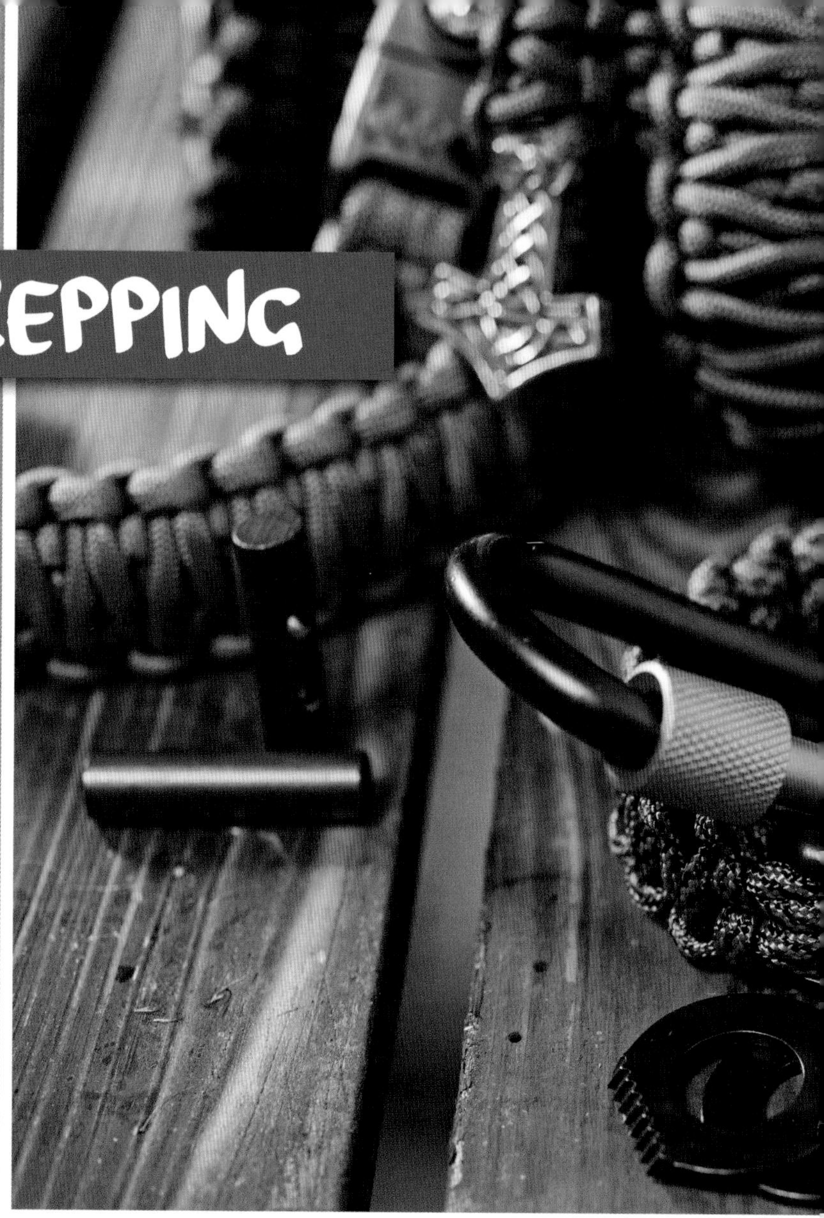

# 1 FUNDAMENTALS OF SURVIVAL

To begin thinking like a survivalist, realize that you cannot control many aspects of your situation, especially past actions, both your own and those of others. You don't have control over the fact that you turned right instead of left, for example, or that it is hot outside, or that a lightning storm is coming. All of those factors are out of your hands. The only thing that you have 100% control over is yourself and what you are going to do in order to improve your situation. So the first thing you need to do is calm down and get your emotions under control. Doubt, fear, frustration, anger, sadness—these emotions cloud your judgment and make choosing the right way forward harder than it has to be. Get rid of them.

Also realize that no matter how fit and tough you are, your natural first response in a survival situation is going to be to panic. The key to getting past panic is to not fight that feeling. Do not try to outrun the emotion. Instead, let the panic pass.

Panicking is a natural reaction in a survival situation, but you can learn to let the panic pass.

# Assess Your Situation

Once you are calm, it is time to assess the situation. I like to think about my surroundings in terms of three zones.

### ZONE 1

**Zone 1 is you.** You need to take into account everything that you have on your person that can be used for your survival. Turn your pockets inside out and take inventory of everything you have. No matter how useless an item may appear, do not discard it. Remember that what you have on you is all that you have to survive.

### ZONE 2

**Zone 2 is the immediate area within your line of sight.** Are there usable resources that you can see within walking distance?

### ZONE 3

**Zone 3 is any area beyond Zone 2.** Typically, unless you are setting up camp for an extended time and may eventually run out of resources, this zone isn't a factor. This is where you explore to find more available resources.

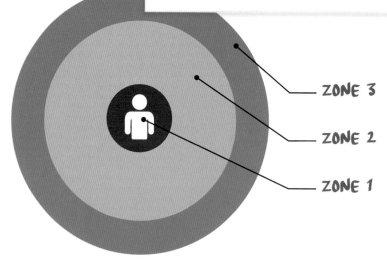

ZONE 3

ZONE 2

ZONE 1

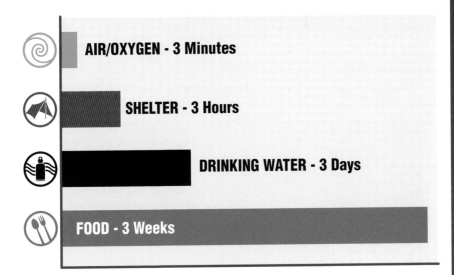

# Survival Rules of Three

Knowing the survival rules of three will help you focus and set priorities. The rules of three are not absolutes; however, they give you an easy way to begin thinking about survival.

1. You can survive **three minutes** without air.

2. You can survive **three hours** without shelter (maintaining your core body temperature).

3. You can survive **three days** without water.

4. You can survive **three weeks** without food.

# The Survival Pyramid

Along with the survival rules of three, another concept to keep you focused is what is known as the survival pyramid. It has three sections.

1. **The base, which is the largest section, is the will to survive.**

2. **The middle section is your knowledge and skills.**

3. **The top of the pyramid, which is the smallest section, is gear and supplies.**

Some people may think this hierarchy is upside down. They're tempted to focus on their gear and supplies. But the most important aspect of a bad situation is your will to survive—your ability to keep putting one foot in front of the other in order to get where you need to be. You could have all the supplies you need at your disposal, but if you don't have the will to survive, the best gear in the world won't help much.

Gear and supplies can be lost or perhaps were never available in the first place. Knowledge and skills cannot be lost or taken away from you. Gear and supplies are last because without the previous two levels of the pyramid, your gear is going to be ineffective.

# Train for the Survivalist Mindset

What if you had to find your own food in the woods and cook it?

Someone once asked me, "How can you possibly be prepared for everything?" The answer is, you can't. But knowing the basics of first aid, navigation, getting food and water, dressing in proper clothing, and how to set up camp will help you in almost any emergency situation.

In addition to learning about survival techniques, it helps to rehearse "What if?" scenarios in your mind. For example, let's say you are in a restaurant and a fire breaks out. What do you do? Do you know where the exits are located? What can you use to break windows or pry open doors if you have to quickly leave the building? Another example: Imagine you are rafting down a river. You hit rapids and your raft capsizes, leaving you stranded without your gear. What is on your person that you can use? Do you know where you can find safety? Training yourself to have a "what if" mindset can prepare you for the unexpected.

Your raft capsizes: now what do you do?

# Stay Prepared with Emergency Kits

It doesn't matter what you are doing or how close you are to civilization, you should always keep a "bug-out bag" for those *just-in-case* situations. It is important to never underestimate the distance between you and safety. With the ease of modern transportation and communications systems, people take too much for granted. They think help will always be available. They will say, "I'm only going fifteen minutes away," or "It's just ten miles away." But I know people who have been stuck in their vehicles overnight in snowstorms, just a few miles from home. Always rely on yourself as your primary means of help and others as secondary.

Here is a list of items that don't take up a lot of room and are easily carried. I consider this the bare minimum of what you should have with you as often as possible.

- **Paracord**
- **A map of your area**
- **Compass**
- **Knife**
- **Multi-tool**
- **Drinking container (I prefer a metal one)**
- **Fire starting kit (lighter, matches, ferrocerium rod, tinder, fatwood— your preference)**
- **Extra set of clothes (weather appropriate for the season and region)**
- **Signal whistle**
- **Tarp**
- **First aid kit**

# 2 ESSENTIAL TECHNIQUES AND TOOLS

**T**here are so many types of knots, bends, hitches, and lashings it's hard to remember them all. However, there are some knots that are especially helpful in a survival situation. They are worth the effort of learning by heart.

It can be frustrating when first learning to tie knots, but regular practice will make it second nature. If you are sitting down to watch TV, have a small length of paracord with you to practice your knot-making skills. Tying knots will eventually become muscle memory, and you will soon tie them without even looking.

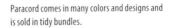

Paracord comes in many colors and designs and is sold in tidy bundles.

# Know Your Knots

### Overhand Knot, page 28

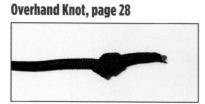

### Overhand Loop, page 28

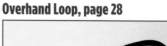

### Manharness Hitch, page 29

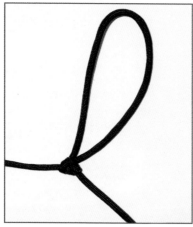

### Fisherman's Knot, page 31

### Bowlines, page 34

### Prusik Knot, page 32

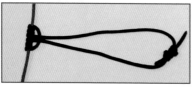

### Running Bowline, page 35

### Triple Bowline, page 35

### Honda Knot, page 37

### Reef Knot, page 38

### Hitches, page 39

### Lashings, page 43

## Overhand Knot

The overhand knot is one of the simplest knots there is. You probably already use it to tie your shoes.

**1.** Even though this is called the overhand knot, I have heard a few people refer to it as the "pretzel knot." Loop and weave as shown.

**2.** Pull the end of the paracord to tighten the knot.

---

**PARA-TIP: Knot Terms**

- **Hitches** tie cordage to an object.
- **Bends** tie two lengths of cordage together.
- **Lashings** tie two objects together.

---

## Overhand Loop

The overhand loop is a very quick means of creating a loop that can be thrown over an anchor point. Double over one end of the paracord and create a simple overhand knot.

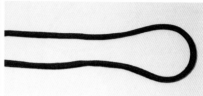

**1.** Bring the end of the paracord around to create a U shape.

**2.** Grab the bottom of the U shape. Fold it over itself and through the middle to create an overhand knot.

**3.** Pull on the loop to tighten the overhand knot.

# Manharness Hitch

This allows a series of non-slipping loops to be made along the length of the paracord.

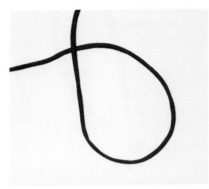

**1.** Twist the paracord one time onto itself in order to create a loop.

**2.** Bring the top left side of the paracord down and lay it across the loop.

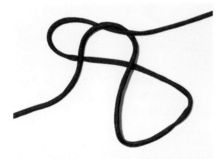

**3.** Twist the bottom half of the loop to create a smaller loop.

**4.** Take the smaller loop you just made and bring it up and through the top loop.

*Manharness Hitch continued on next page*

## Manharness Hitch *(continued)*

**5.** Pull the top loop through and slowly tighten the lower two loops. This is the most important step and needs to be done slowly and correctly. Doing this step incorrectly will result in a loop that is adjustable. Don't worry if you have trouble with this step, it just takes a lot of practice. I still find myself messing this up and having to start over.

**6.** When all of the steps are done correctly, you will end up with a nonadjustable loop like this.

### PARA-TIP: Fashion a Knot-Undoer

Some knots can become so tight that they seem almost impossible to untie. There are several tools that help in loosening stubborn knots, but if you find yourself in the middle of nowhere without any of those tools, you can easily make one from a small piece of wood. Use a cutting tool to sharpen the end of a stick. This end can then be pushed in between knots and used to loosen them. This can save you time and frustration, and prevent you from cutting precious cordage.

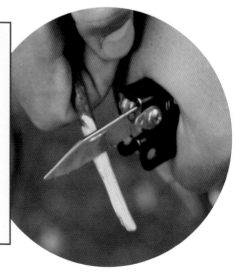

# Fisherman's Knot

The fisherman's knot is a simple way of attaching two pieces of cordage to one another.

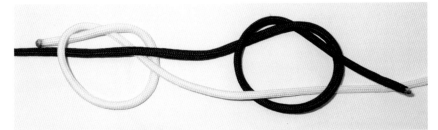

1. Take one end of the paracord and tie an overhand knot around the second piece of paracord. Tie an overhand knot in the same fashion with the other cord. Pull the two lengths of paracord away from each other to bring the knots together. It will help to tighten the first knot when it is made. The picture above is for demonstration purposes.

2. Since these are simple overhand knots, leave a little bit of paracord outside of the knot. This keeps it from coming undone.

## PARA-TIP: Which End Is Which?

When learning knots, there are two terms that come up often that you should be familiar with: the **standing end**, and the **working end**. The standing end is the length of rope that is tied to an anchor, or bearing a load. This is typically the longer length of the rope. The working end is the end of the rope that is being used to tie a knot, or being worked with. It is typically the shorter length of the rope.

# Prusik Knot

The Prusik knot is primarily used among climbers as a safety measure in arresting a fall. The loop with the fisherman's knot is attached to your person. This knot is easily moved up or down the main climbing rope, but when pressure is exerted against it, the knot will grip the rope and not move. This can also be used as a climbing aid in a survival situation. When trying to climb up a rope, use the loop as a handhold to pull yourself up and slide the knot on the main line up as you progress.

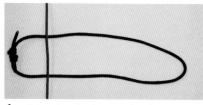

**1.** Take a length of paracord and connect the ends in a double fisherman's knot (pictured with the black paracord). Feed the ends of loop with the fisherman's knot under the main line of cord.

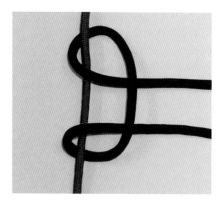

**2.** Pull the left side of the loop, with the knot, over the main line and under the right side of the loop.

**3.** Slightly snug up the paracord and wrap the end of the loop to the left, over and under the main line, bringing it back to where it was. This begins the formation of the loops around the main line.

**4.** Make sure to continuously straighten lines as you go.

**5.** After making three passes, this is what the knot should look like. Be sure to snug this up as much as possible.

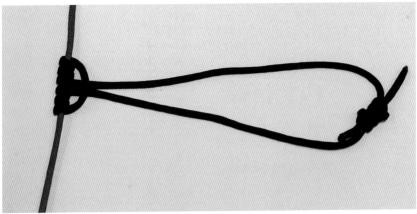

**6.** This is what the Prusik knot with the loop will look like when completed.

# Bowlines

Bowlines make effective nonslipping loops at the end of a line. These can be used for rescuing someone or any other purpose where a fixed loop is needed. Remember that paracord should not be used as climbing rope unless it's an emergency situation.

**1.** Shape the cord like the letter "e."

**2.** Pass the working end up through the loop and under the standing end as shown. Be sure to hold the cut end where you want it so it doesn't become too long after everything has been tightened.

**3.** Pass the working end back down through the loop. Then hold the bottom loop and the cut end of the paracord in one hand while pulling the top single piece of paracord with your other hand to tighten the knot.

**4.** The finished bowline. The fixed loop can be made to any size desired.

# Running Bowline

In order to make a running bowline, first follow the steps to make a bowline (page 34). The long end of the paracord is then passed through the loop.

**1.** You will need to practice making the bowline before attempting different versions of it.

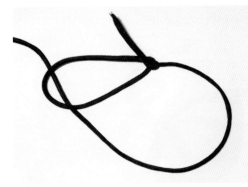

**2.** The bowline can now "run" along the main length of the paracord, creating a larger loop.

# Triple Bowline

The steps in tying a triple bowline are almost the same as tying a regular bowline (see page 34). However, to start you will need to double over the paracord. The end result will produce three loops instead of one. This can be helpful for raising or lowering multiple items of gear.

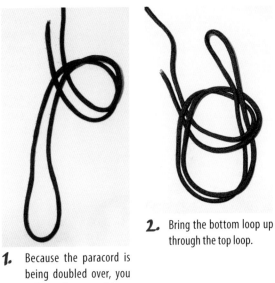

**1.** Because the paracord is being doubled over, you will need more of it to begin with.

**2.** Bring the bottom loop up through the top loop.

*Triple Bowline continued on next page*

# Triple Bowline *(continued)*

**3.** Place the top loop behind the main body of the paracord.

**4.** Bring the loop down and through the middle loop. As this loop is brought through, hold onto the bottom loop as you tighten the knot. In the final step, you will see why this is important.

**5.** By holding onto all of the loops as you tighten the knot, you should end up with three loops of similar size. This may take a little practice to get just right.

## Honda Knot

While you may not be familiar with how to make the Honda knot, I can almost guarantee you have seen it in action. This is the knot that is used to create an adjustable loop, like that used for a lasso.

**1.** Make an overhand knot toward the end of the paracord.

**2.** Make a small loop by passing the end of the paracord back over the main cord.

**3.** Push the cut end of the paracord through the backside of the loop.

**4.** Hold onto the loop you just pushed through with one hand, and in the other hand, hold onto the overhand knot end of the paracord. Pull the loop all of the way through to tighten the paracord onto itself.

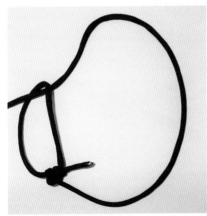

**5.** The final step is very similar to the final step in the Running Bowline (page 35). Pass the longer end of the paracord through the loop, and you will now have an adjustable loop.

**6.** In step 5, the loop that is shown around the main body of the paracord is quite large. I did that for demonstration purposes. Generally, however, I make that loop much smaller. The above picture is more accurate.

# Reef Knot

The reef knot, or the square knot, is used when you want to join two pieces of cordage of the same diameter. Other than the overhand knot, this is probably one of the most well-known knots. I use this knot often, and I think everyone should know it, as it is very simple to make.

**1.** The first step is to take the ends of two pieces of paracord and lay them over one another so that they form an X. Next take one of the working ends and go over and under the opposite cord so that it looks like the picture above.

**2.** Repeat the previous two steps with the working ends so that the same pattern is made above the first one. I used two different colors to help illustrate that the same-color working ends are pointed in the direction of the same-color standing ends.

**3.** Pull the working and standing ends of the same color to tighten the knot.

# Hitches

Hitches are used to attach rope to a pole or post. While there are a variety of uses for hitches, I tend to use them as way of holding the paracord at the beginning or end of a lashing.

## Half Hitch

The half hitch by itself is not all that useful, but variations of it are often used with other hitches or knots.

**1.** To form the half hitch, wrap the working end of the paracord around a piece of wood. Then take the working end under and over the standing end, threading the working end through the loop. From here, simply pull the working end and the standing end in opposite directions to tighten the hitch.

## Clove Hitch

The clove hitch is effective when the load pulling against it is only doing so perpendicular to the hitch. Movements in any other direction tend to loosen the clove hitch. I usually use this as a temporary means of attaching cordage to another object.

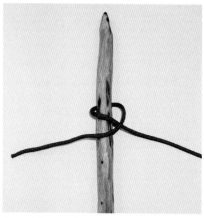

**1.** Make one full turn around the piece of wood with the paracord so that the working end overlaps the standing end.

**2.** Make one more turn around the piece of wood with the working end and pull the end of the cord underneath the top piece.

**3.** Slide the two loops together and pull the working end and the standing end in opposite directions to tighten the hitch.

## Trucker's Hitch

I have also heard this hitch referred to as the canoemen's hitch. It is a useful hitch to know when securing a load or a ridgeline for a shelter.

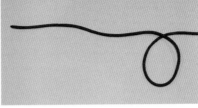

**1.** First create a loop with the working end passing over the standing end to the left.

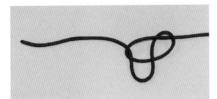

**2.** Next bring the working end under the standing end and through the loop in order to make a second loop. Then pass the working end up through the first loop as shown.

**3.** Pull the working end and the standing end to tighten the loop.

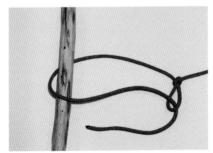

**4.** Wrap the working end around the anchor point, such as a tree. Next, thread the working end through the loop and pull on it as hard as you need to in order to take up the slack in the standing end.

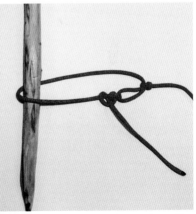

**5.** To finish the trucker's hitch, wrap the working end into two half hitches.

## Timber Hitch

The timber hitch is a quick way of attaching cordage to an object so that the object can be pulled or moved. It can also be used as the beginning of certain lashings, which is what I mainly use it for.

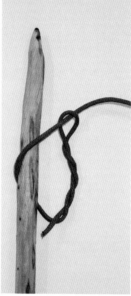

**1.** With the working end of the paracord, make one turn around the object it is being tied to. Then make one turn around the standing end so that it forms a smaller loop.

**2.** Twist the working end of the paracord several times around itself as shown above.

**3.** Finally, pull the working end and the standing end in opposite directions to tighten the hitch.

# Lashings

Lashings are a means of using rope to attach logs or poles together. Knowing how to lash rope is incredibly important for building structures such as a shelter or a raft. (See page 223 for a raft project and pages 176–181 for shelter projects.)

## Square Lashing

The square lashing seems to work best when two pieces of wood need to be secured at right angles to one another.

**1.** On one of the pieces of wood, tie an end of paracord in a clove hitch or a timber hitch. I prefer a timber hitch, but either can be used.

**2.** Next bring the working end up and behind the top piece, over the left piece, under the bottom piece, and over the right piece. Repeat these turns at least three to four times. I kept the turns loose in the above picture to better illustrate the pattern.

**3.** This illustrates the previous step except that the paracord is tight around the wood, as it should actually be.

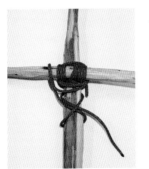

**4.** Make one full turn around one of the pieces of wood and repeat the previous step in the opposite direction. Make sure everything is tight and end in a clove hitch.

**5.** A finished square lashing will securely hold two pieces of wood and can bear a load.

## Diagonal Lashing

Diagonal lashing works best when securing pieces of wood that are not at right angles. An example would be when making an A-frame.

**1.** Tie a timber hitch so that both pieces of wood are within the knot.

**2.** Make several turns in a diagonal pattern in one direction.

**3.** Make one full turn around one of the pieces of wood and continue to make several more diagonal turns over the previous wraps. The crisscross paracord will form an X shape.

**4.** Finish the lashing with a clove hitch.

# Fusing Cords Together

There may be times when you have several lengths of paracord, but what you really need is a single, longer piece. There are several ways you can fuse or tie smaller pieces of paracord together to get a longer piece.

## Fuse with Heat

The first method involves melting two opposing cut ends of paracord and pressing them together for ten seconds. The melted nylon will adhere to itself, and, once it cools, it will be fused together. Be extra careful not to burn yourself when dealing with melted nylon.

This method of fusing and ending paracord is used frequently in crafts and bracelets. While this does make a good bond, it is by no means as strong as the original cord. I caution against using it for anything beyond a clothesline.

**1.** If you have a heat source that you don't have to hold, like a lighter, you can use two hands to hold the paracord pieces. Once the ends turn black and have melted, take the heat source away and immediately press the two ends together. Hold them in place for roughly ten seconds (this cooling time can vary depending on how much material is melted). You can shape the cooling goo to make the bond stronger.

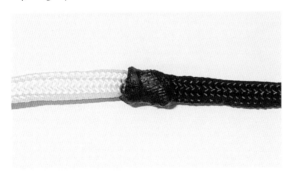

**2.** If the joint doesn't come out to your satisfaction, you can gently reheat the section and reshape. However, sometimes it is easier to cut the section out and try again. Be careful when touching the melted material, because it is extremely hot and sticky.

# Double Sheet Bend

The second method of joining two end pieces is by using the double sheet bend. I like this method because it is easy to remember and it works well with different paracord lengths. You can use this method when tying a yarn to a larger piece of paracord. This bend works well if constant pressure is kept on the joint. When tension is released, though, the paracord can start to untie itself. On the positive side, it is easy to pull apart when you are done with it.

**1.** Take two ends and loop them around each other.

**2.** Pass the end of the white cord under itself and over the black cord.

**3.** Repeat the previous step to double the white cord around the black.

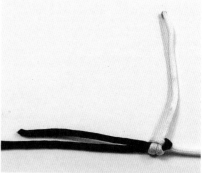

**4.** Tighten the cords and pull the two ends together.

# Double Fisherman's Knot

The double fisherman's knot is a very strong joining method.

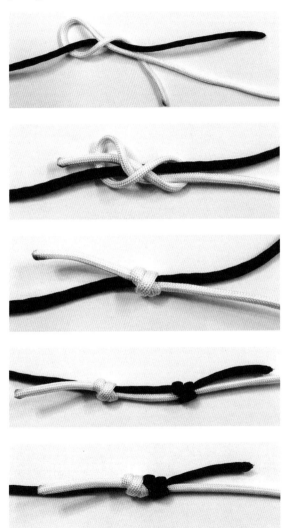

**1.** Using one end, create a loop around the other cord as pictured.

**2.** Pass the end of the white cord back through the two white loops

**3.** Pull the two white ends to tighten the white cord around the black.

**4.** Repeat the above steps with the black end around the white cord.

**5.** Pull the white and black ends in opposing directions to bring the two knots together.

## Sew

The last method is a bit more involved but holds very well. This works best with a threading needle or upholstery needle, but most people don't tend to carry these around. (But if you are carrying paracord, I recommend carrying a few different types of needles in your pack.)

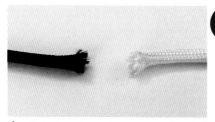

**PARA-TIP: Keep It Sharp**

A sharp cutting tool will always give clean cuts. If a clean cut is not made, the material will fray a lot and the yarns will be sticking out.

**1.** Make two clean cuts, one on each end of the cord. Push the outer sheath back so that about 1–2 in. (2.5–5 cm) of the inner strands are exposed. Then, cut those strands off and pull the outer sheath back up so that the last 1 in. (2.5 cm) of the outer sheath feels hollow. Repeat this process for the other cut end of paracord. The other ends of the cords should be melted and turned into a fine point by rolling the melted ends between your fingers.

Once the hollow ends are in place, cut a hole in one side of the outer sheath that is about ½–1 in. (1.3–2.5 cm) from the end. Thread one pointed end of one piece through the hole of the other piece and pull the strand through, leaving a few inches (about 10 centimeters) on one side.

**2.** Take the melted pointed end of the white cord and thread it through the cut hole and out of the open end of the black cord.

**3.** Take the melted end of the black cord and thread it through the hole and out of the open end of the white cord. Pull the two lengths taut.

**4.** Give the two lengths a good tug in opposing directions. Lightly burn this connection and smooth it out.

**5.** Be careful not to melt too much or the connection will be weakened.

# Helpful Tools for Making Paracord Projects

In this section we will review some of the tools and materials that make working with paracord much easier and more enjoyable.

Pictured below:

 **A** Victorinox Hunter Pro knife

**B** Lighter

**C** Scissors

**D** Ezzzy-Jig Bracelet Maker

**E** Monkey fist jig

**F** Hemostats

**G** EZ Splicer splicing tool

**H** Upholstery needle

**I** Paracord lacing needle

**J** Tape measure

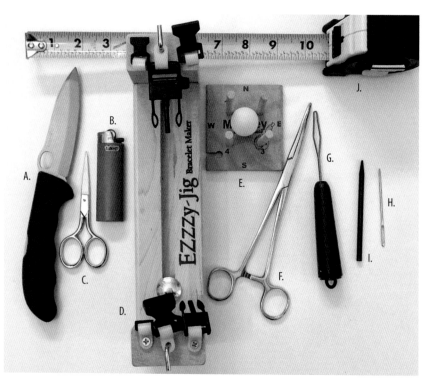

The Essentials:
# Knife and Lighter

The first two tools are very basic
and you should carry them on
your person at all times in the
wilderness: a **sharp knife (A)**
and a **lighter (B)**. The knife is
used to make clean cuts, which
you need when fusing paracord
ends together (see page 45). At

home you can use sharp **scissors (C)** instead of a knife. The lighter is used to melt the
cut ends for joining two pieces of paracord to one another, ending a braid, or closing
off a cut end. (If the end of a cut length of paracord is left open, the inner yarns will
continuously creep out from the sheath as the cordage is shuffled around.)

## Faster Survival Bracelets: Bracelet Jigs

If you plan to make a lot of bracelets, I recommend getting a **bracelet-making jig (D)**.
The jig can be set up with exact measurements, and it securely holds the bracelet
ends, leaving your hands free to braid much faster. I went a number of years making
bracelets without a jig, and I'm glad that I finally got one. You may also want a **monkey
fist jig (E)** (see page 100).

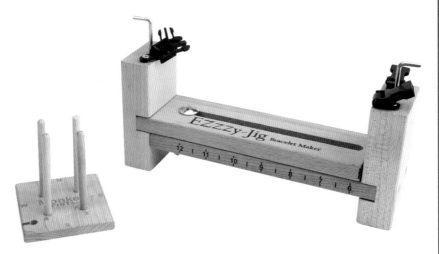

## Needle-Nose Pliers or Hemostats

I also like to have a pair of **needle-nose pliers** or **hemostats (F)** on hand. They help in pulling paracord through tight spaces. They really save time and your fingertips during certain repetitive braids. A **splicing tool (G)** is also very helpful in pulling paracord through knots or tight loops.

## Needles for Sewing and Lacing

These last two tools I not only use at home but also carry in my pack. I carry normal **sewing/upholstery needles (H)** as well as a large paracord **lacing needle (I)**. The lacing needle makes braiding projects so much faster and easier. It consists of a hollow needle that an end of paracord can be threaded into. I find these tools not only speed up the work, but also sometimes make the work possible.

## Tape Measure

You can estimate many lengths, but a **tape measure (J)** will make your work more precise and prevent you from wasting too much extra paracord.

# Useful Accessories and Hardware

There are a variety of accessories for paracord projects, but these are the ones that I use for outdoors and survival projects. First there is the **buckle** or **closure**, used as a means of clasping two ends together for a bracelet, strap, or dog collar. **Plastic buckles (A)** have come a long way in recent years because companies have figured out how to add some cool tools within the buckles. Some have compasses, ferrocerium rods, whistles, and a knife built right into them. However, if you don't mind spending a few more dollars, metal buckles and shackles are much more durable and have more potential uses in a survival situation.

**Crafting beads** can be used to give any project a sharper or more colorful appearance. I use them for pace count beads (see the project on page 216), which some people may know as ranger beads. These are used to judge walking distances when you don't have more advanced technology. **Plastic toggles (B)** can be used in the place of beads, although you would need a number of them for making ranger beads. They are also helpful in gear repair as well as for making pull cord pouches.

**Key rings (C)**, though simple in nature, can help with repairing gear as well as having a multitude of other functions. I always carry a small handful of these in my pack.

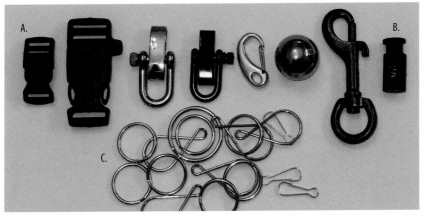

Pictured left to right: buckles (A) (the first is a plain plastic buckle, while the second has a built-in signal whistle and ferrocerium rod), adjustable metal shackle buckles, clasp, 1 in. (2.5 cm) diameter ball bearing, leash clasp, plastic toggle (B), and (at bottom) an assortment of key rings (C) and lanyard hooks.

# Organizing Your Paracord

Not knowing how to properly pack paracord away will give you a tangled, knotted mess and a lot of frustration. Trust me, I have wasted a lot of hours unnecessarily untangling paracord because I just threw it into my pack. In this section we look at some easy ways that paracord can be carried.

These organizers are lightweight, cheap, and available at most stores or websites that sell paracord. You tie one end of the paracord to the frame and simply wrap the rest around it. Their flat shape means they fit well inside a pack. They can also be hung on the outside of a pack. By using one of these wrap organizers, it's easy to hold onto those small lengths, too.

## PARA-TIP: DIY Cordage Organizer

You can make DIY paracord organizers out of common items. For example, take a thick piece of cardboard, like an aluminum foil core, and wrap your paracord around it. The downfall is that when the cardboard gets wet, it will break apart. You can also use a soup or soda can to wrap cordage around.

## PARA-TIP: Organize Your Spare Yarns

In my workshop, paracord scraps have a funny way of finding uses. I never throw anything out. Instead of throwing away the yarns and sheaths and scraps, use an empty sewing thread spool as a yarn carrier. You can keep adding scraps to it by tying the ends together using a sheet bend or a double fisherman's knot. By having this spool of yarns available, you can keep more of your paracord intact instead of gutting it for material.

Most sewing spools have a notch cut into the top, where the end of the thread can be held. You might have to use the tip of a knife to widen it slightly to accommodate the larger yarn.

Some of these carriers are even specifically made for paracord and have a built-in razor for cutting and a holder for a lighter.

# 3 PREP PROJECTS

One of the things that I love about paracord is that you can carry it on you in a functional way while still remaining, dare I say, fashionable? In this section I will show you how to make functional items that you can incorporate into your gear before you venture out into the field. These projects can be made in the comfort of your home so that you will be ready for survival situations later.

Stock up on paracord and start making projects—before things fall apart.

# Quick Deploy Paracord

When seconds matter, you can't afford to sit down and unwind a bracelet or rope to get paracord ready to use. These two quick-deploy projects will give you a handy supplement to cordage that you have tied up in apparel items like bracelets or leashes. They are easy to make and, most importantly, ready at hand in the field.

PROJECT: QUICK DEPLOY HAT (PAGE 59)

PROJECT: QUICK DEPLOY BUNDLE (PAGE 62)

# PROJECT
# QUICK DEPLOY HAT

## WHAT YOU WILL NEED

- 17 ft. (5 m) of paracord

**Estimated Time for Project**

- 10–15 minutes

This project and the water bottle holder (page 93) both use the same braiding method, called the "chain sinnet." The chain sinnet relies on a series of intertwined loops to create the design. The beauty of it is that when cordage is needed, all you have to do is untie the stopping knot and pull on the end. This braided piece, which you can wrap around any field hat, is 17 ft. (5 m) long and when needed only takes four seconds to deploy.

**1.** One reason that I like this braid is that it turns 17 ft. (5 m) of paracord into a length that is just over 3 ft. (1 m), which is much easier to carry. On one end of the cord, tie a simple overhand knot. Make a loop so that the working end of the cord goes over the top of the cord. Bring the working end behind the neck of the loop.

2. Usually I make the series of loops smaller than those displayed in the picture, but if you are just learning this method, it is easier to see what you are doing with larger loops. Taking the working end of the paracord, push it through the first loop to create a second loop. Pull the non-working end of the cord to tighten the first loop down onto the second loop.

3. Here you can see how the first loop cinches down around the neck of the second loop. The bigger the loops are, the quicker the paracord will be used up.

**4.** Repeat the above loop-making steps as many times as needed until you reach the end of the paracord.

**5.** As you progress through this project, the series of loops will begin to look like the links in a chain. When you get to the end of the paracord, stop the loops by simply threading the cut end of the paracord through the last loop and tightening the loop down onto it.

**6.** There can be as much or as little paracord left on the end as you want, as long as there is enough to thread through the last loop. If the final step is ignored, the loops will undo themselves when being moved around.

**7.** To deploy the paracord, reverse step 6 and pull on the cut end of the paracord. This 3 ft. (0.9 m) braided section can be unraveled in four seconds to produce a 17 ft. (5 m) length of paracord.

# PROJECT
# QUICK DEPLOY BUNDLE

## WHAT YOU WILL NEED

• 8 ft. (2.4 m) of paracord

**Estimated Time for Project**

• 5 minutes

Here is the second way to pack quick-deploy paracord. This bundle fits easily in the pocket of a pack. If you strap it to the outside of a pack, it tends to bounce around and unravel. For this method, use most of the same steps involved in the tool handle wrap on page 194. The only difference is that you will be wrapping the paracord around itself instead of around a tool, and you don't fuse the cut ends.

**1.** Take one end of the paracord and create a single open-ended loop. The more paracord that is being wrapped up, the longer/larger the loop needs to be. For this demonstration I am wrapping up 8 ft. (2.4 m) of paracord. Take the working end of the paracord and begin wrapping the loop from the bottom to the top.

**2.** It doesn't matter which direction you choose to start turning the paracord. Depending on the amount of paracord you have on hand, wrap it up and down the body of the loop as many times as needed, making sure not to cover up the top of the loop.

**Make sure that each wrap of the paracord
is nice and snug. All of the turns will have
to be held onto as you wrap this, otherwise
it will unravel before you finish. Eyeball the
amount of cordage you have so that the
wrapping stops at the top of the body. To end
the wrap, you need to thread the cut end of
the paracord through the loop.

**4.** There only needs to be enough paracord left
so that the top loop can cinch down on it.
After the end has been threaded through the
loop, pull on the cut end of paracord sticking
out at the bottom. This will tighten the top
loop and cinch it down. When you need
cordage quickly, just pull the cut end out from
underneath the top loop, and the wrapped
bundle of paracord is easily unraveled.

**5.** The original length of this paracord was
8 ft. (2.4 m) long. When wrapped like this,
it is reduced to a compact bundle several
inches (about 10 centimeters) long that fits
comfortably in my pocket.

# MAKING ROPE

## WHAT YOU WILL NEED

- 400 ft. (122 m) of paracord
- Scissors or knife
- Lighter

### Estimated Time for Project

- 4 hours

For this project you are going to need a total of 400 ft. (122 m) of paracord. Ideally, you will want a spool (1,000 ft. [305 m]) of cord because you will need two separate pieces that are 200 ft. (61 m) each. This project will produce a braided rope that is roughly 75 ft. (22.86m) long, containing 400 ft. (122 m) of intact paracord and an astonishing 3,200 ft. (975 m) of total cordage.

**1.** In these project photos, I refer to the left piece of paracord as "green" and the right piece as "orange." First, place two ends of one piece together and find the midpoint of that piece. Repeat this step for the second piece. Now interlace the two midpoints as pictured.

**2.** Take the top left green strand and pull it down and behind the other pieces. Next bring the piece up in between the two orange strands and over the left orange piece.

**3.** Snug the pieces up so that it looks like this.

**4.** Now we will repeat the above steps but with the orange side. Bring the top right orange strand down and behind the other strands. Bring that strand up in between the two green pieces and over the right green strand.

**5.** Snug up the pieces so the beginning of the rope looks like this. From here, the previous two steps repeat themselves over and over, alternating from the left side to the right side until the rope is the length you want it.

**6.** When done properly, the knots will look like this. After so many knots, the lower section of the cord will begin to weave itself upward and prevent further knots from being created downward. When this happens, just pull the individual strands (the cut ends) out to untangle the mess and begin tying knots again. (It helps to hold onto the bottom section of knots with one hand while doing this to avoid unraveling what has already been braided.)

**7.** When you reach the end of the rope, take all four strands and tie a single or double overhand knot to secure the end. It is quick and easy to make, and just as easy to disassemble when you need the cordage. Do not cut the four individual stands unless they are excessively long. Having them will give extra points for tying off to other objects or gear, or they can be cut to use as cordage while still maintaining the integrity of the rope. If you are having trouble while braiding this rope, it helps to secure the beginning with a table clamp after there are a few inches (about 10 centimeters) tied.

## PARA-TIP: Embellish Paracord Rope

You can find a number of hardware pieces to attach to the top portion of the rope. My favorite is a heavy-duty metal ring or carabiner.

To add this to your rope, braid around the hardware of your choice by inserting it into the beginning loops. When the rope is done, this will make it easier to create loops around something for carrying or hanging purposes.

Having a piece of hardware on the end makes securing the rope to objects much quicker, and you don't have to worry about any knots slipping.

## PARA-TIP: Go Big with Warrior Rope

If you have the time, materials, and patience, I highly recommend making this big brother to the rope discussed in the previous project. The "warrior rope" is kind of my own creation, as I have not seen it anywhere else. (If I am mistaken, I apologize!)

To make this project, you need to first make two separate finished ropes (see previous project). After you have made them, find the midsection of each rope and fold them over. From here, begin braiding the two finished ropes together using the same method as in the standard rope.

The end result is an extremely strong rope with knots that are 1 in. (2.5 cm) in diameter. These knots provide a very firm handhold, even in wet conditions. Given that paracord has some stretch to it, the repeated large knots also act like a suspension system, behaving almost like a bungee cord.

It takes anywhere from ten to twelve hours to finish one of these massive ropes. The other issue is that it cuts down the overall length of the original

You can see that there is quite a difference in the regular rope (right) versus the "warrior" version (left). It requires a lot of work to make, but the end result is worth it.

ropes. The two smaller, finished ropes from the earlier project come in at roughly 75 ft. (23 m) each. Braiding two of those together cuts that length down to a braided rope that is roughly 28 ft. (8.5 m) long, 30 ft. (9 m) including the tails. Still, if you make one of these, you will have 800 ft. (244 m) of intact paracord and 6,400 ft. (1,951 m) total cordage (when broken down to yarns) at your disposal.

# Bracelets

There are two different categories of bracelets that I use in this book: *paracord bracelets* and *paracord survival bracelets.*

A paracord bracelet is made of nothing more than paracord, a buckle, and maybe an accessory. The accessory is usually a metal tag with a symbol on it that means something to the person who is wearing it. While the paracord certainly can be used for cordage in a survival situation, I call these simply *paracord bracelets.*

A paracord survival bracelet, on the other hand, is made up of paracord, a buckle, and other items that are very useful in an emergency situation. This type of bracelet can be customized to contain small compasses, a knife, a whistle, or a ferrocerium rod in the buckle. These bracelets have more to offer in an emergency, which is why I call them *paracord survival bracelets.* The survival bracelet project on page 78 includes fishing line, fishing hooks, jute twine, a button compass, and a ferrocerium rod for starting fires.

**PROJECT: PARACORD BRACELET (PAGE 69)**

**PROJECT: DOUBLE COBRA WEAVE BRACELET (PAGE 73)**

**PROJECT: SURVIVAL BRACELET (PAGE 78)**

## PROJECT
# PARACORD BRACELET

Here's how to make a paracord bracelet that will be 9½ in. (24 cm) long when completed.

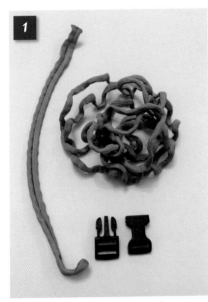

1. The smaller 17 in. (43 cm) length is going to be the core of the bracelet. This project uses a ½ in. (1.3 cm) plastic buckle. First, you must set up the core of the bracelet, which is what you are going to be braiding around. Take the small length of paracord and put the two cut ends together so that the piece is now folded in half. On one end there will now be a loop. Feed this loop through the top of the buckle slot.

2. Feeding the paracord through the slot can be difficult. Use the tip of a pen or something not sharp to help push it through. Feed the cut ends of the cord through the loop.

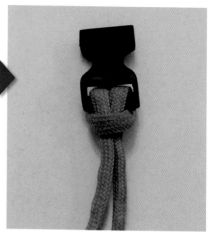

**3.** Pull the cut ends all the way through the loop and snug it up against the buckle. This is called a cow hitch (aka lark's head).

Lark's Head Knot

**4.** Now it's time to create the body of the bracelet. This is the beginning of the cobra weave. Take the long length of paracord and put the two cut ends together so that the piece is now folded in half. On one end there will now be a small loop. That is the midpoint of the cord. Place this behind the core of the bracelet.

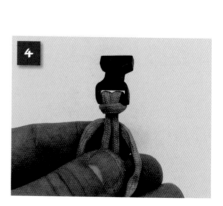

**5.** Take the left side of the cord and place it over the core and under the right cord.

**6.** Everything can be loose at this point. Take the right cord and go under the left cord, behind the core, and up and through the left loop.

**7.** Basically, this is an overhand knot that is repeated many times. Pull the left and right cord taut so that it produces a knot. This knot does not have to be extremely tight. Once you know how to make the first knot, you are going to repeat this process for the rest of the bracelet, just alternating the steps.

**8.** For the second knot, take the right cord and place it over the core and under the left cord. It is starting to take shape.

**9.** Take the left cord and place it under the right cord, behind the core, and up and through the right loop. Getting the hang of it?

**10.** Pull the right and left cord taut to make the knot. Go back to step 5 and repeat these steps until you reach the end of the bracelet.

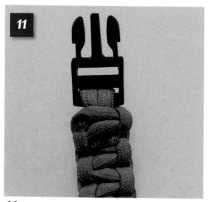

**11.** Once you get to near the end of the bracelet, feed the two cut ends of the core through the top slot of the other buckle. Fold these ends back onto the core and finish the braiding around the ends. When you can't braid any more, cut all of the loose ends close to the bracelet. Use the lighter to melt the ends.

**12.** Your finished bracelet will look like this.

# DOUBLE COBRA WEAVE BRACELET

This bulkier bracelet offers more cordage, which comes in handy in survival situations. The double cobra weave is also used in the survival bracelet project on page 78, so making this will be good practice.

For this project I used a plastic buckle that houses a signal whistle and a ferrocerium rod for fire starting. Before you begin, measure your wrist. An easy way to do this is to take a length of paracord and wrap it around your wrist, then use a ruler to measure that piece. My wrist measures 7½ in. (19 cm) around when the cord is tight, but tight bracelets are uncomfortable and I need to allow for some room for the buckles to bend around and close. Since the double cobra weave will make the bracelet thicker, I added another 2 in. (5 cm) to the total length. From end to end the bracelet measured 9½ in. (24 cm) long.

While not necessary, a bracelet jig can make the process much easier, especially if you're a beginner. Measure the long piece of paracord and make a cow hitch (lark's head) loop around one of the buckle ends. Thread the working ends of the paracord through the top of the other buckle end.

## WHAT YOU WILL NEED

- 150 in. (381 cm) length of paracord
- 17 in. (43 cm) length of paracord
- Plastic buckle
- Lighter
- Knife
- Ruler
- Bracelet jig (optional but recommended)

### Estimated Time for Project

- 15 minutes

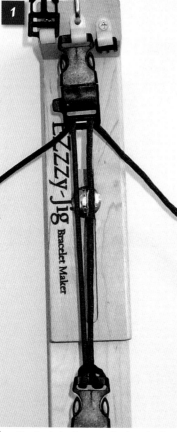

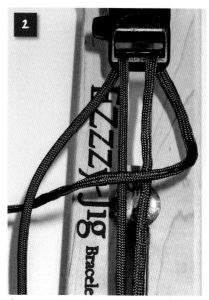

**2.** To start the braiding, take the working end of the purple piece, and place it over the two middle strands and under the far left green piece. Fold the left green strand under the purple piece, behind the body, and up and through the purple loop on the left side.

### PARA-TIP: Stick to Cobra Weave

There are many different braiding styles out there for making a bracelet, but I always come back to the cobra weave. It is one of the easiest styles to learn, easy to disassemble, versatile, and it doesn't take that long to complete a project using this style. It's my braid of choice.

**1.** The body is the strands that the braid is being made around. The working ends of the paracord are the ones you braid with. It doesn't matter if the cow hitch loop is on the top or bottom.

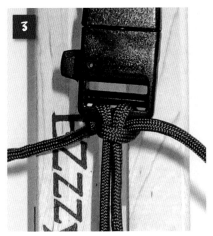

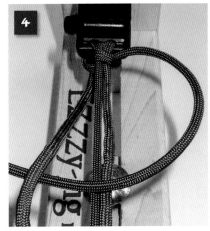

**3.** Pull the working ends of the green and purple ends in opposite directions to tighten the knot.

**4.** At this point make sure that the body of the bracelet spanning the jig is taut. Bring the green strand over the body and under the leftmost purple strand. Take the purple piece and bring it under the green strand, behind the body, and up through the right green loop. Pull the working ends of the green strand and purple strand to tighten the knot.

**5.** With the jig, repeat the steps on the same side—but it will soon alternate. At this point you are probably getting tired of the repetition, but you are almost at the end. Take the left green piece and place it over the body and under the right purple strand. Take the working end of the purple strand and place it under the green piece, behind the body, and up and through the green loop on the left side.

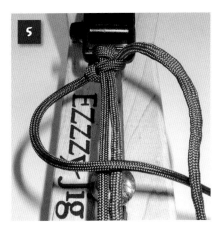

6. This is the intermediate step between each knot. Pull the working ends of the green and purple pieces in opposite directions to tighten the knot.

7. Here is the beginning of the cobra weave! Repeat the above steps, alternating from the left to right side until you reach the other buckle.

8. When you get to the end of this step, you can choose to do one more knot if you want to cover up the splice section. However, I like to leave a bit of leeway between the knots and the buckle. This allows for some give when trying to bend the buckles to clasp them. At this point, rotate the jig 180 degrees so that the top of the bracelet is now at the bottom.

**9.** The zigzag Vs and the top alternating loops let you know that you are doing the braid correctly. Begin braiding downward in the same manner as before, starting with crossing the right working green strand over the body. As you progress with the double cobra weave, note that as the green strand is tightened over the body, it rests between the previous layer of purple loops.

**10.** At first the double cobra weave feels awkward to braid, but after a few turns it will begin to feel more comfortable. When you get to the end, cut the loose ends and melt them back to the body of the bracelet.

## PROJECT
# SURVIVAL BRACELET

Since we're adding gear items to this survival bracelet, having the jig hold the body of the bracelet really helps. The Ezzzy-Jig is very user-friendly. The top and bottom part of the jig is held together by a bolt and wingnut, allowing it to slide in and out depending on the size of the bracelet you are making. There are numbered markings on the side that indicate the length of the bracelet in inches. On the ends of the jig are two plastic buckles of different sizes secured to the jig. Between these buckles there is a small metal rod that acts as an empty spot where you can use any kind of buckle you want. Since the buckle that I am using is different than what came with the jig, I will be using the middle slot. It is important to note that when you are using a different style of buckle, you will need a pair of them. The first set is used as anchor points to the jig and the second set is what the bracelet will be braided to.

I like to use the double cobra weave braid, because it is simple to make and to disassemble, and it provides quite a bit of cordage. For the clasps, there are a number of options, but I mostly use plastic quick-release clasps that are lightweight and easy to undo. The second clasp is a metal shackle. The metal shackle is heavier and can be a little harder to undo. I like the metal shackle because, after the bracelet has been taken apart, the shackle can have

a lot of other purposes. The third option is to use no clasps at all and to simply secure the bracelet via a knot and loop. I don't really like this method because it is not very secure. The last kind of clasp I have used and will be using in this project is a plastic buckle with a built-in fire starter and a signal whistle.

## WHAT YOU WILL NEED:

- 20 ft. (6 m) of paracord
- Fasteners for the closers
- Scissors or knife
- Lighter
- 20 ft. (6 m) of fishing line
- Fishing hooks
- Jute twine
- Button compass

### Estimated Time for Project

- 30 minutes

1. Measure your wrist. My wrist is 7 ½ in. (19 cm) around, but I needed to add another 1 ½ in. (3.8 cm) to accommodate the thickness of the bracelet.

2. Fold the 20 ft. (6 m) long piece of paracord in half and find the midpoint. Thread the midpoint through the end of the plastic buckle and make a cow hitch. You will notice in the picture that I use two different colors of paracord that I spliced together. This makes it easier for you to see and follow the steps, but it's better to use one single cord instead of two for a genuine survival bracelet. Take the cut ends of the cord, thread them through the top of the other buckle, and pull them through.

**3.** When making a double cobra weave on a jig, start at the top and work your way down. Pass the working end of the dark green cord over the top of the two strands and under the working end of the orange cord.

**4.** It's okay if the two strands spanning between the buckles are a bit loose at this point— we will fix that in a minute. Now, take the working end of the orange cord and go under the left green cord and behind the body, then up and through the right green loop.

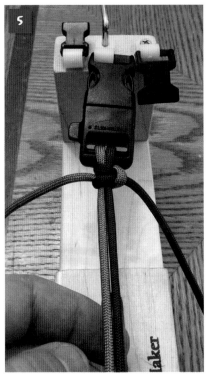 

**5.** Remember that when I say the "body," I am referring to the paracord pieces that I am braiding around. Pull the orange and green cords in opposite directions in order to tighten the knot. Don't make it too tight, though, because the two strands in the middle (the body) need to be pushed upward before you snug the first knot into place.

**6.** Once there isn't much slack in the body of the bracelet, go ahead and tighten the knot and push it up close to the buckle. Repeat the previous steps one more time. Pass the green cord over the body and under the orange cord. Pass the orange cord under the green cord, behind the body, and up and through the left green loop. Pull the green and orange cords in opposite directions in order to close the loops and make the knot.

**7.** The knots do not have to be overly tight, but it's good practice to push each complete knot up so that it is snug with the previous one. The previous step will now be reversed each time you make a knot. Take the green cord and pass it over the body and under the orange cord. Pass the orange cord under the green cord, behind the body, and up and through the green loop. Pull the green cord and the orange cord in opposite directions to tighten the knot.

**8.** The paracord running down the middle of the body should be making a V shape, which is a sign that you are doing the method correctly. Continue the previous steps until you get to the other end of the bracelet. It should look something like the picture.

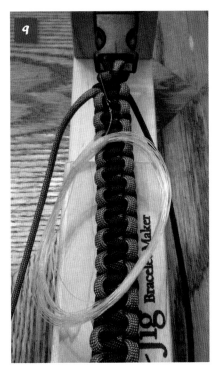

**9.** To braid this bracelet in the double cobra weave, you need to undo the buckles and rotate the bracelet 180 degrees so that what was the bottom is now the top. The fun part is just about to begin, because you will now add the elements that turn this paracord bracelet into a paracord survival bracelet. Measure out 20 ft. (6 m) of fishing line and tie a hook to one end. Coil the fishing line up and hold it together with a few small pieces of tape. Stick the hook into the cow hitch, just below the buckle. From here continue braiding downward like you were before, but make sure the fishing line is kept in the middle of the bracelet.

**10.** I'll admit that incorporating the fishing line can be a bit frustrating, but just take your time. In a real survival situation, this fishing line could really come in handy. The double cobra weave creates an interesting design and in this case protects the fishing line very well.

**12.** Using 30 in. (76 cm) of jute twine and a splicing tool, thread the twine into the top orange loops of the bracelet. Jute twine is a very cheap and effective material to use as tinder for fire starting, which is why I like to incorporate it into some of my projects. After pulling the first piece of jute through, tie the end of it in an overhand knot to the loop you pulled it through. Continue pulling the twine through every top loop in a zigzag pattern until you get to the other end of the bracelet. When you thread it through the last loop, tie that end of the twine in a simple overhand knot as well. When adding the jute twine, only add it to the top of the bracelet—jute twine is very itchy against the skin. This bracelet has a lot to offer: almost 160 ft. (49 m) of total cordage, a signal whistle, a ferrocerium rod for starting a fire, jute twine to use as fire tinder, a compass, and 20 ft. (6 m) of fishing line with a hook. Now that is a bracelet fit for the wilderness!

**11.** You almost can't even tell that there is 20 ft. (6 m) of fishing line in the center of this bracelet. You could finish up the braiding, cut the ends, and melt them closed. But this is a survival bracelet—keep adding things to it! On the second-to-last knot, add in a clip-on button compass (good to have as backup for your main compass). It slides right onto the paracord. Then finish the braid, cut the ends, and melt them closed.

PROJECT
# DOG LEASH

## WHAT YOU WILL NEED

- 75 ft. (23 m) of paracord
- A dog leash clasp
- Scissors or knife
- Lighter

### Estimated Time for Project

- 2 hours

Who better to share your outdoor adventures with than your best doggy friend? Many people I have made these for tell me they prefer the feel of the paracord dog leash over store-bought ones. When broken down, this dog leash will provide 600 ft. (183 m) of cordage.

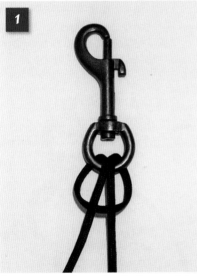

**1.** Measure and cut a length of paracord that is 12 ft. (3.6 m) long. Fold this piece in half and make a cow hitch around your desired hardware. I use a standard dog leash clasp.

**2.** Take a 63 ft. (19 m) long piece of paracord, fold it in half, and place the midsection behind the body of the leash. Splice and join a length of black and green for the braiding.

**3.** Place the left side of the cord over the body of the leash and behind the right cord.

**4.** Place the right cord under the left cord, behind the body, and up through the left loop.

**5.** Pull the cord through and tighten the knot.

**6.** Repeat steps 3 and 4 but in reverse. Place the right cord over the body of the leash and under the left cord. Place the left cord under the right cord, behind the body of the leash, and up through the right loop (shown in the picture for step 7).

**7.** Here you can see the knot before tightening. Pull the cords to tighten the knot. Repeat steps 3 and 4 for the majority of the leash.

**8.** After several wraps, the leash will begin to look like this.

**9.** Once my fingers are exhausted, I know I am nearing the end. At this point there is about 8 in. (20 cm) of the leash body left. From here, flip the end of the leash over.

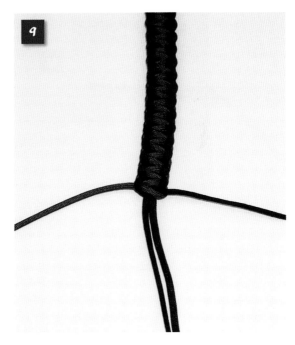

**11.** As you move downward, make sure to keep the inner two strands in the middle of the braids. After braiding roughly 4 in. (10 cm), take the inner two strands and fold them up and back onto the leash. Spin the leash around so you can continue braiding downward.

**10.** I flip the end over to a pre-marked spot. From this spot to the clasp of the leash is 4 ft. (1.2 m). From here, continue braiding downward. This will result in a double cobra weave braid.

**12.** Once you get to the bottom of the leash loop handle, you are done braiding. All of the paracord ends can be cut and melted with a lighter to finish up.

# PROJECT
# EQUIPMENT SLING

## WHAT YOU WILL NEED

- 70 ft. (21 m) of paracord
- 31 in. (79 cm) of 1 in. (2.5 cm) nylon webbing
- Two sling swivels or hardware of your choice: carabiners, shackles, etc.
- Two buckles
- Cutting utensil
- Lighter
- Sewing machine (optional)

### Estimated Time for Project

- 2 hours

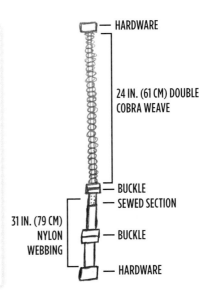

From top to bottom: hardware of your choice, 24 in. (61 cm) of braided double cobra weave, sliding buckle, 31 in. (79 cm) of nylon webbing with the first 2 in. (5 cm) overlapped and sewed, sliding buckle, hardware of your choice.

This type of sling is my favorite one to make and is quite popular. A sewing machine is not required, but it will make a portion of this project much easier. I, however, don't mind a bit of hand sewing to keep my skills honed. This project requires you to do the cobra weave.

Measure out 70 ft. (21 m) of paracord and fold it in half. Slide the desired hardware (sling swivel) through one of the paracord pieces and push it all the way to the midpoint of the cord. Grab the sliding buckle and thread both of the cut ends of paracord through one of the slots. The sliding buckle should be 2 ft. (61 cm) from the end shackle. I shortened this distance for the picture so that you could see the placement of the hardware.

People who have liked this design have asked me if this could be made into an all-purpose sling, and it certainly can! All you need to do is swap out the hardware on the ends of the sling. For this sling I will be using a metal shackle so that I can use this as an all-purpose adjustable sling. If you want it to be a rifle sling, thread the paracord through the sling swivel pictured at the top right in the photo instead of the shackle.

**1.** The hardware (top left: metal shackle, top right: sling swivel, bottom: plastic buckle) is in place, so it is time to start braiding. For the paracord that is threaded through the sliding buckle, fold over so that the body of the braid will be the 24 in. (61 cm) section between the buckle and the shackle. Take the left cord, place it over the body, and under the right cord.

**2.** Take the left cord, place it over the body, and under the right cord. Then put the right cord under the left cord, behind the body, and up and through the left loop (pictured in step 3).

**3.** Pull the left and right cords to tighten the knot. The second knot will use the same steps but reversed. Put the right cord over the body and under the left cord. Then put the left cord under the right cord, behind the body, and through the right loop. These steps alternate for every knot that is made.

**4.** Here is what the sling looks like with the first two knots tied. Continue braiding like this until you reach the end of the 24 in. (61 cm) section. Now let's make it a double cobra weave. Turn the sling 180 degrees so that the shackle is now on top. Continue the braiding all the way back down the body. Once you reach the buckle, cut the working cords off and use a lighter to melt the ends.

**5.** Here is the beginning of the double cobra weave. The paracord part of this project is done, so now it's time to make it adjustable. Measure and cut a length of nylon webbing that is roughly 31 in. (79 cm) long. After cutting the nylon, use a lighter to melt the frays, just like the paracord.

**6.** Thread an end of the nylon, webbing through the opposite slot in the buckle that the paracord is tied to. Fold over roughly 2 in. (5 cm) of the webbing back onto itself.

**7.** With the two sections of nylon webbing pressed together, sew the 2 in. (5 cm) overlap. I use a very simple running stich with some variation to it. My sewing technique is very primitive but it works. There is still a little more to do. Thread the cut end of the nylon through both of the slots on the last buckle and slide it up. Thread the cut end of the nylon through the last hardware piece (sling swivel). Bring the cut end of the nylon back up to the buckle and thread it through the backside of two slots of the buckle. By moving the nylon webbing through the buckle, it can be adjusted to your liking. At its shortest length the sling is roughly 32 in. (81 cm) long but can be adjusted out to 41 in. (104 cm).

**8.** After threading the webbing through the last piece of hardware (the sling swivel), be sure to loop it back up and through the underside of the sliding buckle.

PROJECT

# WATER BOTTLE HOLDER

A benefit of making this project is that the water bottle can be removed and the wrap can be used as a container for other items. This wrap has a lot of paracord that can be used for cordage that deploys very quickly—100 ft. (30.5 m) of whole paracord or a little over 800 ft. (244 m) of broken-down paracord. It also works well as an insulator and protects the bottle from damage. The chain sinnet design is used here.

## WHAT YOU WILL NEED

- Water bottle
- 110 ft. (33.5 m) of paracord
- Scissors or knife
- Hemostats (needle-nose pliers can be substituted for these but hemostats work much better)
- Lighter
- Toggle (optional)

### Estimated Time for Project

- 2 hours

**1.** Cut a length of paracord that will go around the very top of the bottle that you will be braiding from. The length of this piece doesn't really matter as long as it goes all of the way around the bottle with a few inches (about 10 centimeters) to spare. I like to make mine a bit longer because I like carrying as much cordage as I can. The piece that I am using is 24 in. (61 cm) long. Thread the two cut ends of this piece through a toggle and cinch it up around the bottle. If a toggle isn't available, tying both strands into an overhand knot will do.

2. Take the working end of the long length of paracord and tie an overhand knot to the collar piece that goes around the bottle. Slide it over next to the toggle. On this overhand knot, leave about a 1 in. (2.5 cm) tail, which you feed into the toggle merely to hold the knot in place. With the working length of paracord, feed a piece of it up and under the collar piece so that there is a loop on top and a U-shaped loop on the bottom.

3. Make sure there is a bit of slack in the collar piece of paracord so that you can easily slide the working end under it. The collar is going to slip and slide a bit as you initially work on this. Fold the top loop down over the collar while still leaving a small lower loop by the overhand knot.

4. Make sure that the overhand knot does not become inverted while doing this step. Place the working end of the paracord through the loop that was folded over, in order to create another loop.

**5.** This feels a bit tricky at first, but soon you will get a feel for it. Next, pull the left base of the folded loop down behind the collar; this will tighten the first loop you made. You should now have something that resembles bunny ear loops.

**6.** Pull the top strand of the right loop. This will close and tighten the left loop, creating the knot in this braid.

**7.** We are now essentially back to step 1 and will repeat this process. Bring the loop up and under the collar piece.

**8.** Fold the loop down and over the collar piece.

**9.** Bring the working end of the paracord behind and through the loop.

**10.** Pull the lower left base piece down again to create the bunny ear loops. Pull the top strand of the right loop in order to close and tighten the left loop.

**11.** Repeating the previous steps will produce the chain sinnet design. The first round of knots around the collar should be just a little bit loose and spaced out. This will allow for the top to be cinched shut if the water bottle is taken out later on and you decide to use it to carry other items. Throughout this braiding process, the loops should only be snug and not overly tightened. Once you have made knots all the way around the collar, you will reach a stopping point at the toggle and it will look like the picture. This is when you are going to need to start using the hemostat tool.

**12.** From here on, the working end of the loop is going to need to be fed through the loops that are on the bottom of the above row. The first loop you will go through is the one created just after the overhand knot.

**13.** Insert the hemostat tool. Push the tip of the hemostat through the top of the first loop and use it to grab the working end loop. Pull the working end loop up and through the lower loop.

**14.** This is why you do not want to overtighten the loops. If they are too tight, trying to open the hemostat to grab the lower loop is almost impossible. After many, many loops, you will finally reach the bottom of your container.

**15.** At this point, as you make the loops, press them down and over the edge of the bottom of the container. As you continue on, the loops will spiral inward toward the center of the bottom. Because of this, at some point, it will be difficult to thread the working loop through the loop in the row above it. To overcome this, feed the working loop through every other loop above it, instead of every single one.

**16.** Almost done! Once the spiral has made its way to the center of the bottom of the container, no more loops can be made. If need be, cut the working end of the paracord so that there is as much length as the height of the water bottle. Thread this end through the last loop and pull it to close the loop down. This will cinch the loose end.

**17.** When you are at the end, make sure to leave one last loop. For the last step, take the water bottle out of the paracord container so that the container is empty. Thread the cut end of the paracord through the centermost hole in the bottom and push the remaining length through so that it is hanging out of the opening of the container. Grab this piece with one hand and give it a firm tug. This will invert the last loop/knot by pulling into the container, leaving a flat bottom. The strand you just pulled can be dropped into the container and the water bottle can be placed right on top of it.

**18.** Having that handy loop at the top allows for the bottle to be hung anywhere. To break down the water bottle holder for cordage, take the water bottle out of the holder and stick your hand inside. Press the knot on the bottom and the remaining paracord strand back through to the outside of the container. Untie the last knot that was made and start pulling the loose end. By pulling on this strand, it will untie the loops you made in a single motion, very easily. When you have the desired amount of cordage, cut the paracord and tie off the end onto one of the loops to keep it from unraveling.

# PROJECT
# DRAWSTRING POUCH

## WHAT YOU WILL NEED

- A piece of material for the pouch or a tin soup can if making it entirely out of paracord
- 85 ft. (26 m) of paracord
- Knife

### Estimated Time for Project

- 2 hours

Having a small pouch as a carrying container provides a number of benefits. For this project, I use only paracord to make a pouch. Like the water bottle holder, this project is made with the chain sinnet knot. When you know what size of pouch you want to make, find an object that is of similar dimensions—a water bottle, soup can, or soda can are good options for forming the frame of the pouch. This pouch will fit in your pocket or hang on the outside of a pack.

The main difference between making the drawstring pouch and the water bottle holder is how the first row of knots is made. In order for the pouch to close as tightly as possible, the first row of knots needs to be spaced apart quite a bit. Since every pouch size is different, you will just have to experiment by tying the first row, sliding it off of the can, and seeing how it closes. For the pouch pictured here, I used 85 ft. (26 m) of 325 paracord to wrap around a typical soup can.

**1.** Note how loose and how far apart the top knots are from one another.

**2.** With a little bit of paracord and time, you can make yourself a handy container for collecting wild edibles and fire tinder, and for keeping all of your important items safe.

# PROJECT
# MONKEY FIST

The "monkey fist" is just a way of tying rope or cordage that results in a ball of material. I like the monkey fist because it adds weight to the end of a line for throwing purposes. For that reason, I prefer to wrap the monkey fist around a 1 in. (2.5 cm) diameter steel ball bearing. This gives some nice weight to the fist when throwing a line over a tree branch or from a boat to shore. While this project can be made without a monkey fist jig, I prefer to use the jig because it just makes the process much easier.

**1.** Measure out 10 ft. (3 m) of paracord, then cut and melt the ends to make it easier to work with. On one end of the cord, measure up 2 ft. (61 cm) from the cut end and tie an overhand knot. The jig that I am using has a slot in it where I can slide the knot in. This helps to keep that portion of the cord from unraveling while I wrap the paracord around the jig. Make five full wraps around all four posts of the jig. As you come around for what would be a sixth wrap, take the cord and pass it over the top of the bottom two posts going to the right side of the jig. This will be the beginning of the horizontal wraps. Make this first round of wraps before you place the ball bearing between the posts.

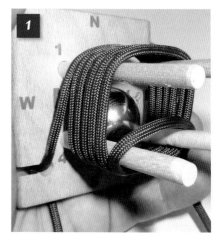

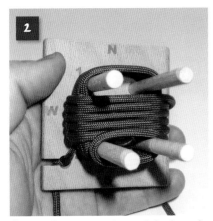

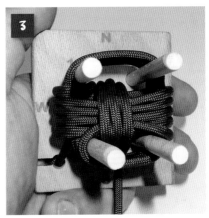

**2.** The first horizontal wrap helps keep the ball bearing from falling out. The horizontal wraps are now going to be made in a counterclockwise pattern. Take the cord that went over the bottom two posts and feed it behind and around the first layer of wraps, working your way upward. Make five full wraps, ending the fifth wrap by threading the working end of the paracord just inside the upper left post of the jig

**3.** Don't make the wrappings on the jig too tight. Keep them snug, with a little bit of wiggle room to work with. Next, wrap the final and inner layer. Starting at the top left post, thread the working end of the paracord through the top gap from the front to the back. Push the cord down behind the back horizontal wrap and through the bottom gap so that it comes out of the front. Repeat this over-and-under wrap five times.

**4.** It is now time to carefully pull the monkey fist off of the jig. To do this, place your fingers so that they are between the back jig frame and the monkey fist. Then use a scooping motion to hold everything together as you slide it from the wooden posts. You should now have what appears to be a rough-looking monkey fist. Don't worry—we're going to tidy it up.

We need to tighten all of these loose wraps around the core. In order to do that, first turn the monkey fist in your hand so that the cord with the overhand knot is on the top and pointing out and to the left. This will be what I call the beginning or the start side.

Pull this cord just enough to slightly tighten the beginning part of the wrap. Follow this cord to the right and you will see certain strands tightening. Work your way down the wraps in a back-and-forth pushing-and-pulling motion to tighten the wraps. You will need to turn the monkey fist in the appropriate direction in order to follow the wrappings. As you move along, you will create excess cordage that, when you get to the end cord, will pull out of the monkey fist wrappings. Complete this as many times as needed in order to bring all of sides down around the core. The trick to this is to take your time, tighten the sides evenly, and tighten the sides just a little bit every turn. I went through this process about eight times before I was satisfied with the wrappings.

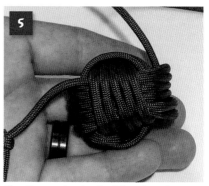

**5.** Your monkey fist should be taking shape and look similar to the one pictured.

### PARA-TIP: Take Your Time

The key to making a great monkey fist is taking your time and making sure that all of the sides are as even as possible. When wrapping around a core, if the sides are not even there is a chance that the core could slip out one of the sides.

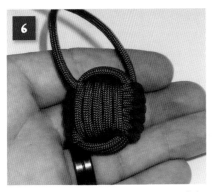

**6.** After taking this picture, I went around the fist two more times, tightening the wraps. Don't make the final go-around too tight, because then wrappings start to get pulled in too much and the core begins to show.

**8.** With the excess paracord that was cut off from the handle, make a double cobra weave braid around the looped handle. To be able to use the monkey fist as a weighted end for rope line, double the looped handle over and tie a length of paracord to the loop. Then throw the line. The cobra weave reduces the amount of open space in the loop that could get caught on another object. The loop makes it easier and quicker to attach a length of paracord to.

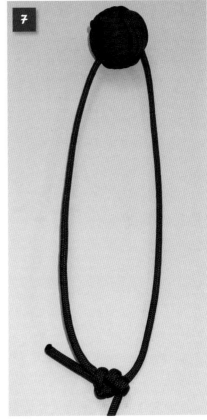

**7.** Now it's time to make a handle for your monkey fist. Take the two single strands of paracord, measure them to a 12 in. (30 cm) length, and cut. Melt the ends and then tie them together in a double fisherman's knot to create a looped handle.

# PROJECT
# MULTI-TOOL POUCH

Pouches that can be made from paracord are very versatile. The pouch in this project is a little different because it is going to be made for one particular tool. This project is a multi-tool pouch with a fold-over top for one of my favorite gear items, my Victorinox Swiss Champ. The required amount of paracord that I list here is specific for this tool. If you are making a pouch for a smaller or larger tool, you will have to adjust the amount of paracord accordingly, using the method described in step 1.

1. The first order of business is to measure out the frame of the pouch. To do this, take a length of paracord and wrap it around the perimeter of the tool and then double that length up. On one end, tie an overhand knot to create a small loop. This section will need to be long enough to fold over the top of the tool so that it can be secured in the finished product. Then cut the cordage on the right side of the step 2 picture 1 in. (2.5 cm) or so above the Swiss Army Knife. This piece is roughly 12 in. (30 cm) long.

**2.** It's okay that the cordage is not extremely tight around the perimeter. In fact, it should be a tad loose. Take the 11 ft. (3.3 m) piece of paracord and braid a cobra weave around the 12 in. (30 cm) section. When you get to the end of this braid, cut the black cord ends and use the lighter to burn them back onto the body of the braids. There should be about 1 in. (2.5 cm) of the green tails sticking out past the cobra weave.

**3.** Here is what the main body of the frame should look like after completing step 2.

**4.** Wrap the completed frame around the multi-tool and double-check the measurements. This one ended up being a little bit larger than I intended, but that is better than being too small. It is now time to use the paracord threading needle and start weaving the checkered sides of the pouch. Thread the needle onto one of the 4 ft. (1.2 m) long precut pieces. Four feet (1.2 m) is actually a bit much, but it's better to have too much cordage than not enough.

**5.** With the Swiss Army Knife sitting in between the sides of the frame, insert the needle into one of the black side loops near the top and across the knife to the other side of the paracord frame. When the frame is held like that in the picture, the side loops that you thread through are the ones on top facing you. The needle is then threaded through a side loop on the right side that is directly across from the left loop. Pull the majority of the cordage through but leave a few inches (about 10 centimeters) of cordage hanging out of the side.

**6.** Leaving a few inches (about 10 centimeters) of cord hanging out of the side of the frame will help out later in the project. Continue the weaving process by going down the pouch using every side loop. Keep the paracord loose as you weave it—you do not want to make the cord tight yet.

**7.** The tool doesn't have to remain in the frame during this process, but it helps to maintain proper orientation. Once you get toward the bottom, press down as much as possible to flatten out that portion of the frame. Then thread the needle through a side loop but instead of going across the frame, it is now time to weave upward. Thread the needle through the horizontal wraps in an over-under fashion (see step 8).

**8.** It may be helpful to remove the tool at this point, but remember to periodically return it to check the sizing. After getting to the top, reverse the weave and head back down the side of the pouch. To help get the parallel cords out of your way, use the tip of the threading needle to push them to the side.

**9.** It's okay that the lines don't look pretty yet. You will deal with that at the end of the project. Continue the up-and-down weaving until you have gone through the last side loop on the bottom. Just like the top, leave a few inches (about 10 centimeters) of paracord sticking out of the last loop. This side is done, so now flip the pouch over and repeat step 8 for the other side.

**10.** With the sides in place, use a pair of hemostats to pull all of the cord snug. If you don't have a pair of hemostats, the tip of the needle can be used instead. Leave the tool in the pouch so that you don't tighten the sides too much, causing the multi-tool not to fit in the pouch. Again, don't pull the cordage tight, but just snug enough that the lines are straight. This is the reason why I left a few inches (about 10 centimeters) of cord hanging on the outside of the frame: it makes the straightening process easier. After everything is straight, cut the loose ends and burn them back onto the body of the frame.

**11.** It is now time to add the finishing touch—the plastic toggle. Fold over the top and place the leftover tails hanging from the body through the loop. To keep the top secured, thread the tails through a plastic toggle and tighten. There are various hardware items that you can add to customize the pouch, like carabiners or key chains. If you want to get creative, you could even braid some belt loops onto the side.

**12.** Voila! There is a bit more of a gap at the top than I would have liked, but the pouch is snug enough around the Swiss Army Knife that there is no way it is going to fall out on its own.

### PARA-TIP: Cord Colors

Chose your cord colors carefully. If the pouch is ever dropped, certain colors will stand out well against natural backgrounds so it doesn't become lost.

# SURVIVING

**A**t this point, you know something about paracord and how to make useful everyday items with it. Now it's now time to explore what can be done with that paracord when your adventures don't go according to plan. Paracord is one of the most versatile tools to have in the wilderness. So roll up your sleeves, because it's time to put that paracord to work!

# 4 FISHING AND HUNTING

**P**eople can actually survive about three weeks without food, according to the rules of 3 (see page 19). However, since most of us have enough food to eat as often as we like, we quickly notice the signs of not consuming enough calories: headaches,

fatigue, and the inability to focus. As hunger worsens, it becomes harder and harder to accomplish tasks that are crucial to survival. For primitive fishing and some forms of hunting, paracord is invaluable when searching for that next meal.

Fishing can be a great way of catching your next meal because it usually doesn't require nearly as much energy as hunting. Depending on the type of animals in the area, fishing can also be a much safer way to get food. Throwing a line and hook in the water doesn't pose as many dangers as going after something that can bite you.

It can be very frustrating seeing a fish nearby that won't take the bait or come any closer to you. Try your best to not let this consume you and try to find comfort in the fact that this is how our ancestors survived. Even though we have become accustomed to a certain way of life, know that in the wild everything doesn't happen instantly. There is a great satisfaction in waiting for an end result.

Paracord is naturally slick and doesn't always grip the best against itself when used for certain knots. Being wet doesn't help, so be confident in how your paracord is tied when used for fishing.

Some forms of hunting can be achieved using paracord as well. Just be sure you can handle whatever prey it is you're trying to catch and eat.

# PROJECT
# FISHING WITHOUT HOOKS

## WHAT YOU WILL NEED

- Paracord yarns
- Bait

### Estimated Time for Project

- A few minutes, because all you are doing is tying a few overhand knots in the line

Unless you are in a real predicament, wild fish must be left alone.

If you find yourself in a survival situation with no fish hook, you can tie a piece of bait to the end of a line and make a few overhand knots near the bait, about 1 in. (2.5 cm) apart. If you use only gentle tension—not jerking on the line—it may work out that fish swallows the bait and the line and that one of the overhand knots becomes lodged inside the fish. DO NOT practice fishing this way outside of a survival situation, as this method is harmful to fish.

**1.** Break down your paracord and pull a single yarn out. The smaller yarn gives you more options in terms of the size of fish that can swallow it.

**2.** Your best bet for bait is going to be an earthworm, insect, or berry. The bait needs to be secured to the end of the yarn but not so tight that yarn will cut through it. It only needs to be tight enough to ensure the bait and the yarn is swallowed. Remember that it takes patience and a very light touch.

### PARA-TIP: Paracord Yarn Is Enough

A whole piece of paracord is too large to use for fishing. A single yarn piece is small enough to thread through most fishing eyes (if you are lucky enough to have manufactured hooks on hand) and is strong enough to reel most types of fish, including those weighing 8 lb. (3.6 kg) or more.

# FISHING WITHOUT A POLE

## WHAT YOU WILL NEED

- **Paracord yarns**
- **Hook**
- **Bait (optional)**
- **An object to wrap the yarn around: stone, piece of wood, water bottle**

### Estimated Time for Project

- **5 minutes**

A fishing pole is nice to have, but a natural pole can be too bulky to carry in a survival situation. Creating a smaller fishing kit that is easier to carry is simple and requires less energy. Use any small object that is suitable for wrapping a long length of paracord yarn around. This can be rock, a water bottle, or a small piece of wood. I used a small piece of wood that I was whittling. The nice thing about using wood is that you can secure the sharp end of the hook by gently pressing it into the wood.

1. Secure the yarn around the object. A few simple overhand knots should suffice.

2. Next wrap the majority of the yarn around the object; this acts as a fishing reel. You should use 15 ft. (4.5 m) to 20 ft. (6 m) of yarn as fishing line, but it really depends on what you are fishing for and where. The remaining end of the yarn should hold the fishing hook and a weight if you need one (a small stone can be used for the weight).

3. When you are ready to fish, unwind as much of the yarn as you think you can throw out into the water. Remember to hold onto the object that the yarn is secured to! You reel in the line by wrapping it back around the object.

4. When you are finished, simply wrap all of the line back around the object and tuck the hook under the yarn. This little fishing system will store nicely in a pack or even one of your pockets.

## PROJECT
# FISHING HOOKS

### WHAT YOU WILL NEED

- Materials to shape a hook from
- Paracord yarns
- Knife

### Estimated Time for Project

- 30 minutes

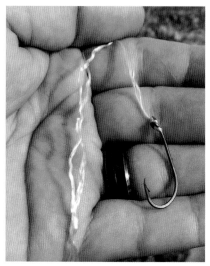

If you don't have a factory-made fishing hook like this, you can improvise your own.

While it would be great to have factory-made fishing hooks on hand, you can catch fish using improvised hooks. The best materials to make hooks from are thorns, wood, and bone. Here is a simple hook that I will show you how to make out of two pieces of wood. This technique shows how to bring two materials together for a hook. They don't have to be made from the same material. A piece of wood could be used for the shank and a large thorn from a plant could be used for the hook portion, if need be.

This is going to be a rather large hook, but this is so you can see the different parts easily. I think I will hang onto it in case I find myself fishing for a monster fish someday!

### PARA-TIP: No Bait? Don't Give Up

Obviously, you will have much better luck hooking a fish if the hook has some kind of bait on it. But you can catch fish on hooks that have no bait. It usually takes much longer, and it takes some luck, but don't give up. Throw the hook into the water, because you never know!

1. Shave down the two pieces of wood into the right shape and size. On one end of each of the pieces, cut a slight angle so that they fit together into the shape of a hook

2. Cut a small notch all the way around the top of the shank so that the fishing line can be properly secured to the hook. Next, tie a piece of yarn to the end of the wood piece that will be the hook. Be sure to tie it to the end.

3. A couple overhand knots will help to hold the yarn in place while you wrap the rest of the hook together. Place the two ends of the wood pieces together so that they can be wrapped together. You don't want any of the yarn to come between the two pieces at this point. Nylon is slick and any yarn between the wood pieces will allow them to move. It's okay to have a small portion of the hook piece overlapping the shank piece.

## PARA-TIP: Use Found Hook Material

You don't have to use only natural materials when it comes to fashioning a fishing hook. Coming across trash in the wild is not that uncommon, and if you use a little imagination, hooks can be made from these items.

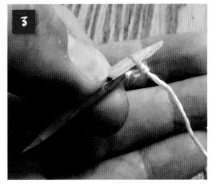

**4.** This photo is included to show what this step should NOT look like, because paracord can slide around, and this step can be easily overlooked. To bring these two pieces together, make one loop around the hook and shank piece, followed by one wrapping around the shank piece. This step is repeated many times until you work your way up the pieces. Each and every one of these wraps needs to be as tight as you can make it in order to hold these pieces together. As you progress, periodically check the rigidity of the two pieces. When you are convinced that it will hold, that is your stopping point. Because paracord can be slick and you don't want these two pieces to come apart, there is a certain way to end this. When you are done wrapping horizontally, make a couple very tight vertical wraps around the middle of the paracord. This will cinch the horizontal wrap tighter and hold the two pieces even better.

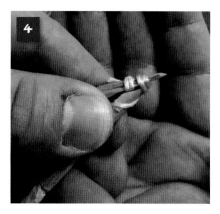

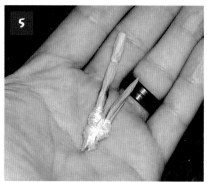

**5.** This hook may look a bit hokey, but it will catch fish.

## PARA-TIP: Enjoy the Hook-Making Process

Knowing how to make fishing hooks from natural materials is an important skill. But I have also found that making them is very relaxing and rewarding. You can carve fishing hooks at home at the end of the day or around the campfire. It's a great way to unwind while still prepping!

PROJECT
# PARACORD LURES

## WHAT YOU WILL NEED

- Length of paracord
- Fishing hook
- Scissors or knife
- Lighter (optional)

### Estimated Time for Project

- 30 minutes

While live bait works best, sometimes it can be hard to find. In a survival situation, you may not want to spend the energy or time searching and collecting it. Luckily, it is easy to make lures from paracord that are quite effective. These work best with larger fish. Scale the size of the lure up or down depending on the type of fish you observe.

**1.** The lizard lure, made from scraps of paracord, works well with bass. First choose a length to use for the body. At one end tie a few simple overhand knots onto each other to give the appearance of a head. This will also give the lure a bit of weight. Next, take a small piece and attach it to the body with an overhand knot. On each end of this piece, tie another overhand knot and make a cut past the knot leaving a small end of paracord exposed. The front legs are now complete. Fluffing up the ends gives more movement to the lure when it is in the water.

**2.** The next step is to make the lizard body. Use a piece of paracord that is roughly 12 in. (30 cm) long and begin braiding it with the cobra weave design. Fold the 12 in. (30 cm) section in half to find the midsection. Place the midsection behind the body of the orange piece. Take the right green cord and go over the top of the orange body and under the left green cord. Take the left green cord and go behind the orange body and up through the right green loop. Pull the left and the right green cord in opposing directions to tighten the knot.

**3.** To continue the cobra weave, reverse the previous step. Take the left green cord and place it over the orange body and under the right green cord. Then place the right green cord behind the orange body and up through the left green loop. Pull the left and right single green cords in opposite directions to tighten the knot. Repeat these steps five or six times to get the size that you want.

**4.** To finish the lure, tie two simple overhand knots on the left and right green cords and then cut any excess paracord, leaving a small amount past the knots. The body and the back legs are now in place. For the tail, leave about 1 in. (2.5 cm) of the original orange cord and tie an overhand knot in the end, cutting any excess off but leaving a bit after the knot. This lure is now ready for a swim!

## PARA-TIP: Disguise the Paracord Smell

Paracord, especially brand new paracord, can have a distinct smell. This could discourage fish from biting. After making a lure, rub it in the dirt or rub fish guts on it in order to get rid of that smell.

## PROJECT
# FISH TRAP

### WHAT YOU WILL NEED

- Sticks
- Paracord

**Estimated Time for Project**

- 1½ hours

In a survival situation, when you are hungry, you are not going to be picky about what kind of fish you bring back to the campfire. This project has two parts. The outer cage is the frame of the entire trap and acts as the holding pen for the fish. The second, and probably more important part of this trap, is the opening. The opening is going to start out large but be reduced in size on the inside of the trap, creating a bottleneck. This is so that the fish can enter but will have much more difficulty trying to escape.

1. A green piece of wood works best for the frame of the opening because it needs to be circular. To shape a green piece of wood without breaking it, gently bend it in the direction that you want many, many times in order to loosen up the fibers. Once you can make a circle, tie the two ends together to keep it in place.

2. Cut several long branches that will be used for the rest of the frame. The length and number of branches depends on the size of the trap that is being made. But there should be enough branches so that fish cannot escape through any gaps between the pieces. Begin tying one end of each of the branches around the circular opening. It's best if they are placed on the outside perimeter of the opening so that they maintain their strength.

**3.** Allow the opposite ends of the side branches to fall in until they come to a point. Close off this end by weaving paracord in an over-under fashion through the wood.

**4.** The main body of the trap is complete, but you need to add one more thing to keep the fish in. Take several sticks and sharpen one end of each into a spear point. Tie these sticks along the inside perimeter of the opening, with the spear end pointing inward. This fish trap can now be put to work.

**5.** This trap works well in streams or rivers where there is a running current. Put the trap in a spot where it can be wedged or weighted into place. Build a small wall out of rocks on both sides of the opening in a V shape. This will serve two purposes. The rocks will help to direct fish into the trap. The rocks can also increase the water flow into the trap, creating a vacuum effect. When emptying the trap, it may be necessary to push a few of the inward spikes down into the trap to create a larger opening.

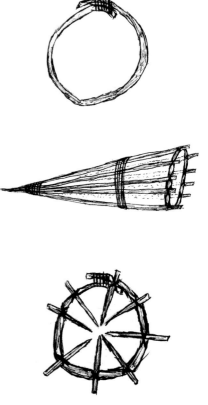

**PARA-TIP: Don't Let It Float Away**

Creating a fish trap takes time, materials, and a possible meal that you may never get back if the trap floats away. It is worth the extra effort to tie one end of the trap to an anchor point in case the current knocks it loose.

## PROJECT
# FISH LINES

### WHAT YOU WILL NEED

- Lengths of paracord
- Paracord yarns
- Several hooks
- Knife

**Estimated Time for Project**

- 30 minutes

Setting out fishing lines is another way to inactively catch fish so that other tasks can be attended to in the meantime. Small rocks can be tied just above the hooks to act as sinkers.

The longer your paracord is, the more hooks you can add to it, which increases the chances of catching a fish. Measure out enough paracord so that you can stretch it across the water between two anchor points on either shore. Then take out all of the inner yarns. Cut the yarns into sections of a few feet (about a meter). On each strand of yarn, attach a hook and tie it onto the outer sheath of the paracord. Place the hooks several feet (about a meter) apart from each other. After you bait the hooks, the line is ready to be set up. There are two setup options (see box at right).

**Option 1.** String it horizontally across the water and anchor the two ends.

**Option 2.** Attach a weight (such as a rock) to one end of the line and throw it into the water. Make sure you are holding onto the opposite end so that all of the line doesn't get pulled into the water. Anchor the end you're holding to a tree or rock. This method is easy to set up, and by varying the lengths of the baited lines, you can catch different kinds of fish.

## PROJECT
# FISHING NET

A fishing net can be used as a primary fishing tool by sweeping it through the water, or it can be used to scoop a hooked fish out of the water. It can also be used as a net to catch other kinds of animals or as a mesh bag in order to carry other items. If you take the time to make a quality net, you will find out how useful it is and may wonder how you ever did without one.

**1.** First decide how big of a net you want to make. The net in this project will be roughly 5 ft. long by 5 ft. wide (1.5 m by 1.5 m)—not so big as to make carrying it difficult, but big enough that it can be used for a variety of purposes.

**2.** Cut a 5 ft. (1.5 m) long piece of paracord and lay it horizontally on the ground. If you prefer to stand while making the net, this length can be tacked to a wall or a tree. I call this piece the "top."

**3.** Measure and cut the individual sections that will be secured to the top and tied to one another in order to make the body of the net. Use an even number of sections, fourteen in this case. Each section is made up of 15 ft. (4.5 m) of paracord that is folded in half. Each time a knot is tied, some length will be lost, so keep that in mind when trying to figure out your dimensions.

**4.** Once you have your sections cut, it is time to begin tying to the top piece. The first step here is to fold the 15 ft. (4.5 m) sections in half. Then tie the two end pieces first and secure them with an overhand knot. When you secure the ends, use all three strands of paracord to tie the overhand knot.

**5.** A cow hitch (aka a lark's head) will be used to attach the yarns to the top piece. To tie the cow hitch, fold the paracord over the top section so that it makes a loop. Then pull the two working strands through the loop and snug it together. The rest of the sections are added to the top piece with a cow hitch. After all of the sections have been tied to the top paracord piece, space them out at equal distances from one another by sliding them along the paracord.

**6.** Here is what the cow hitch should look like on the black paracord section hanging down. Now it is time to start making the body of the net. Start in the center and work your way out. When you have found the center, grab the right strand from the left section and the left strand from the right section. Pull these two pieces tight and make an overhand knot.

**7.** It doesn't matter if you move from left to right to finish the row, but you really need to finish a whole row before moving down to the next one. I tend to move to the left, so that is how I explain it. Take the single green strand on the far left and the right black strand from the next section over, and tie an overhand knot. Before tightening up the knot, do your best to make sure that the knots are in line with each other. Continue these steps until you reach the left side. When you get to the left side, you can tie the side knot now or wait until the next row. It's better to tie one now because it gives you an idea of where the next row of knots is going to go.

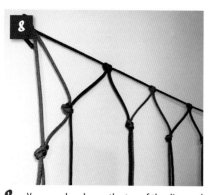

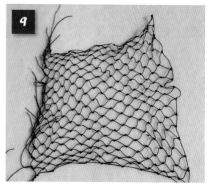

**8.** You can already see the top of the diamond shapes that will make up the rest of the net. Move back to the center and continue tying the knots in the same fashion to the right until the row is done. Always complete the entire row before moving down to the next. Tying the knots in this manner will produce diamond shapes for the body of the net. This is how you will know you are on the correct path. Make sure that the knots are tight, but keep an eye on how tight you are pulling the hanging paracord strands together. Pulling them too tightly will pull in the sides of the net and the overall width will begin to diminish.

**9.** As you may be able to tell, my finished fishing net is not exactly to the dimensions I planned, and it's a little lopsided, too. This is because I didn't take my time. The net is certainly still functional for what it's for, however. Cut another 5 ft. (1.5 m) piece of paracord and lay it out along the bottom knots. Then use the excess paracord after each knot to tie a series of overhand knots with this 5 ft. (1.5 m) section along the bottom border. If you want it to look nicer, go ahead and cut the excess off and use a lighter to melt all of the ends.

### PARA-TIP: More Cordage for Smaller Fish

The more knots you make and the smaller you make them, the smaller the diamond shapes or holes of your net will be. This requires more cordage, so plan ahead. But if after using the net you find that the diamonds are too large and are letting fish through, you can also use yarns to weave additional cordage through the net in order to make the gaps smaller.

# PROJECT
# FISHING ROD

## WHAT YOU WILL NEED

- A pole for the rod
- Paracord yarns
- Fishing hook

### Estimated Time for Project

- 20 minutes

As long as you have paracord, you have fishing line, and with a solid piece of wood and about 20 ft. (6 m) of yarn, you have a decent fishing pole. A strand of inner yarn makes a great substitute for fishing line and is probably one of the strongest fishing lines you will ever use. Find a branch that is at least as long as you are tall. Branches that are around a ½ in. (1.5 cm) in diameter and that do not taper off toward the tip are best. The thinner the branch is, the more likely it will be to snap when a fish is on the line.

### PARA-TIP: Use the Right Wood

Make sure that the branch you are using is green so that it has some bend to it, or is dry and solid, so the branch doesn't break under the weight of a caught fish. In a survival situation, you don't want to miss out on a potential meal.

1. Wrap the yarn around the length of the pole and then tie it off at the end. The pole doesn't have to be completely wrapped in line, however: eight to ten wraps is enough to maintain an anchor for the rest of the line.

2. For the tip of the pole, wrap the line loosely around to form a few loops, then thread the remainder of the line through the loops. Even if the tip of the pole is broken off, the line won't be lost because it is wrapped around the length of the pole.

PROJECT
# FISHING SPEAR

## WHAT YOU WILL NEED

- One branch, roughly 5 ft. (1.5 m) long
- Three smaller pieces of wood
- Paracord yarns
- Knife

### Estimated Time for Project

- 25 minutes

1

**1.** From left to right: the spear body, two spear points, and a barbed spear point. When all three pieces of wood have been completed, place them around the larger branch at equal distances from each other and tie it all together with the yarns. Once the spear end is completed, it can be used as is.

While they are effective fishing tools, spears require patience in their making and in their use. If you make a spear with multiple prongs, your chances of striking and holding onto a fish increase. On the three smaller pieces of wood, use your knife to carve pointed ends and a few barbs. Taking the time to properly carve barbs will be helpful in holding onto a fish when it is speared.

**2.** To help hold the first spear point in place, it helps to tie a knot around the bottom of it. Wrap the yarns a few times around the larger stick and put the second spear piece in place. Once the second piece is secured, add the last piece and continue wrapping.

**3.** Use a hollowed outer sheath to cover the yarns and to finish wrapping the spear. Unless you are in still, shallow water, where retrieving the spear is easy, I suggest tying a long length of paracord to the blunt end so that you can retrieve it after it has been thrown.

## PARA-TIP: Aim Lower than What You See

Water bends light; when you see an object in the water, it is not exactly where you think it is. You may have noticed this at a swimming pool when a person is standing halfway out of the water. Their body doesn't look perfectly aligned with the part that is above the water. Because of this effect, the fish is usually sitting lower in the water than you think. When you throw a spear, aim slightly below the fish.

# PROJECT
# SIMPLE ROCK SLING

## WHAT YOU WILL NEED

- Two strands of paracord, roughly 3–4 ft. (0.9–1.2 m) long
- A piece of material for the pouch, such as leather, cloth, etc.

### Estimated Time for Project

- 10 minutes

This tool is very easy to make and at first glance easy to use. However, it takes a lot of practice and patience to use effectively. As a boy, I made one of these and became quite good at using it. A few broken windows and some spankings later, I had to give up my trusty sling, at least until I hit adulthood. It is a very worthwhile skill to acquire, because it is an effective tool for stunning small game such as birds, rabbits, and squirrels and for knocking other food sources down from trees. The ammunition is plentiful—rocks are everywhere! You can use any rock, but the rounder and smoother the rock is, the better it will fly.

The first few times I tried using a rock sling ended pretty badly. Without any prior experience, I whipped the sling around my head as fast as I could and released the rock. I had zero aim, so I hit a few vehicles, broke my mom's birdhouse, and smashed a window. When you're starting out, swing

1. Cut two small slits/holes, one on each side of the piece of material. Thread the cordage through the cuts and tie off into a knot.

2. On one end of the cordage, tie a small loop.

3. To use, place a rock into the pouch while holding the ends of the cordage in one hand. Slip the loop around your fingers. Swing the sling in a fast circular motion, and then let go of the loose cordage end, releasing and propelling the rock toward the target. The loop around your fingers allows you to keep hold of the sling itself.

the sling only fast enough so that the rock stays in the sling. This way, you can get a feel for the proper release point. Once you can actually aim the rock, you can start building up your speed.

# PROJECT
# WOVEN ROCK SLING

## WHAT YOU WILL NEED

- 15 ft. (4.6 m) of paracord
- Cutting tool

### Estimated Time for Project

- 40 minutes

It's time to go very old school and make a David and Goliath rock sling. This woven rock sling is composed of two lengths of paracord that connect to a small pouch. It is used just like the basic rock sling (see page 130). Like a bola (see page 134), it takes a bit of time to hone your aim. Practice by using a dead tree stump as a target before setting out on the real deal.

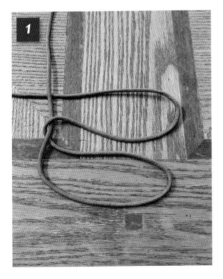

**1.** Measure and cut roughly 15 ft. (4.6 m) of paracord. Take one end of the cord in your left hand and hold it tight while stretching your arm out to the side. From your left hand to the middle of your chest is the length that you want for this section. This will end up being one of the two handles for the sling. Lay this section out with the cut end pointing upward and the end of the measured piece directly in front of you, as this is where the sling braiding will begin. After the measured point, form two loops as shown; I make them about as long as my hand. (In the picture, the strand running off to the left is the working end.) These two loops are going to be used as the frame for the sling pouch.

**2.** Bring the working paracord strand (from the left side) over the top of the shorter strand that is laid out vertically. Pass the working strand under the top strand of the top loop, up through the loop, over the bottom strand of the top loop, under the top strand of the bottom loop, up through the loop, and over the bottom strand of the bottom loop. After every pass, push the strand you are threading through snugly to the left.

**3.** Step 2 is the basis for the braiding of this entire project. Make another pass, this time working from bottom to top. Pass the working end under the bottom strand of the bottom loop, up through the loop, over the top strand of the bottom loop, under the bottom strand of the top loop, up through the loop, and over the top strand of the top loop. You should be able to see the pattern of the pouch begin to take place.

**4.** Repeat this weaving pattern along the length of the original two loops. Your pouch should now be looking like mine in the picture. If you want the center of the pouch to be wider than the rest of it, don't pull the working end too tightly along that section. The two ends will naturally be pulled together, but you can begin putting more tension on the working end as you near the end of the two loops. If you want, use the tip of a paracord threading needle to help push the finished passes together snugly. This will help to make the pouch more pleasing to the eye, but more importantly will reduce gaps where rocks could get hung up.

**5.** To finish the pouch, thread the working end of the paracord in between the two loops and under the last weaving pass that you made. Cinch all of this tightly and tie an overhand knot. After taking this picture, I added two or three more weaving passes to the pouch before ending the weave, but it was easier to show you the end knot like this when it was still somewhat loose.

**6.** Bring the two ends of the paracord together and cut off any excess so that the ends are the same length. These two pieces are the handles of the sling. Toward the end of one of the handles, tie a simple overhand knot (as I have done) or a small loop. When using the sling, either put the loop around your fingers or put the knot between two fingers, and hold onto the loop or knot when your release the loose end when "shooting". This allows the pouch to open and throw the rock in the desired direction without you losing your grip on the entire sling.

**PARA-TIP: Practice Makes Perfect**

Just like with the bola (see page 134), if you don't take the time to practice with this sling, you will have a lot of frustration and some sore spots. When I first started using this sling, I was throwing rocks that were breaking windows and hitting myself in ways that created some nice bruises. Take the time to properly learn how to use your tools in order to avoid mess and injury.

## PROJECT
# BOLA

## WHAT YOU WILL NEED

- **Three strands of paracord, roughly 2–4 ft. (0.6–1.2 m) long**
- **Weights, such as rocks or wood**
- **Knife**

### Estimated Time for Project

- **30 minutes**

A bola can be a great hunting tool to ensnare animals and birds, and it doesn't require a lot of time or raw materials to make. You can use from 2 to 4 ft. (0.6 to 1.2 m) of cordage to make yours; any longer will make the bola too difficult to use.

Use brightly colored cordage on the bola—it may be thrown in areas of tall grass or other environments that could make it difficult to find.

1. Find three rocks or pieces of wood that are roughly the same size, shape, and weight. Wooden bolas cannot be thrown as far, nor will they impact the target as forcefully as rocks will. However, they are still effective and can be a safer way to train when first practicing.

2. Measure and cut the cordage. Tie each rock or piece of wood to one end of the lengths of cordage by either weaving a small pouch around the rock/wood or securing it with a knot. If you want to use rocks but are having a hard time wrapping the cordage around them, try wrapping them in a small piece of fabric to make a pouch, which can then be tied off to the cordage much more easily.

3. Take the opposite ends of the cordage and secure them all together by either weaving a small handle or tying them together in a knot.

4. It's time to practice using the bola. Hold onto the bola by the end with the knot, allowing the weights to hang down. Begin spinning the bola around above your head. When you are ready to throw it, let go of the handle when you can feel the weight of the bola coming around to the front of you. It takes practice to get a feel for the proper release point, so try not to get discouraged. As it hits the target, the momentum of the weights should wrap the cordage around whatever it hits. The idea is that the cordage will wrap around the legs of an animal or the wings of a bird so that is immobilized. Sometimes the weights themselves can stun or even kill the target.

# PROJECT
# BASIC SNARE

## WHAT YOU WILL NEED

- At least 3 ft. (0.9 m) of paracord
- Three pieces of wood
- Knife

### Estimated Time for Project

- 15–20 minutes

When I think of traps, the first thing that comes to mind is a snare. A basic snare is a piece of cordage or wire with one end tied into a loop. When an animal attempts to go through the loop, the loop tightens on itself and traps the animal.

When setting up a snare, try to place it in a location where animals are likely to be walking. Look for a spot where the grass has been worn down or for a small opening in heavy vegetation. Game trails may be easier to see if you lie down so that you are looking at ground level—try to think like a rabbit! Once you have found a good location, making the frame and snare itself is quite easy.

1. The frame consists of three pieces of wood. Cut a notch into two pieces of wood toward one end and press the opposite end of these pieces into the ground about a foot away from each other. The notches need to be facing in opposite directions. The last piece will be the crossbar. Carve notches into this piece so that they line up with the side pieces, then place the crossbar.

2. Tie a section of the cordage in an overhand knot around the crossbar, leaving enough cordage to create the hanging loop. Hang the loop so that it is in the direct path of where the animal is going to walk. The loop needs to hang loosely so that it can tighten when the animal becomes ensnared in it. Make sure that the non-loop end of the snare is firmly anchored to another structure.

3. To help funnel the animal into the snare and not around it, add dense piles of brush or additional standing pieces of wood along the sides.

# PROJECT
# SPRING SNARE

## WHAT YOU WILL NEED

- **At least 3 ft. (0.9 m) of paracord**
- **Knife**

### Estimated Time for Project

- **30 minutes**

A spring snare is a little more complicated than a basic snare (page 135). It includes an anchor and a trigger stick that is attached with cordage to a bent sapling. When an animal becomes tangled in the snare, it releases the trigger, and the sapling straightens up, pulling and tightening the snare. Key to this snare design is finding a useable sapling as close to a game trail as possible (see the basic snare description on page 135).

**1.** Find two pieces of wood to use as the anchor and the trigger. On one end of the anchor, carve a spear point; on the other, cut a notch. Pound the spear end firmly into the ground. Cut a notch into the trigger piece of wood that corresponds to the anchor notch so that it can hook into the anchor notch while positioned upright.

**2.** Make an overhand knot snare as described for the basic snare, then attach the end of the snare to the top end of the trigger. Tie the rest of the cordage to a nearby sapling, bending the sapling over to create tension, and then hook the notch of the trigger into the notch of the anchor.

**3.** Lay out the snare loop, using another piece of wood if needed, to set the trap. Be sure that the cordage is firmly tied off to both the trigger and the sapling so that it will support the weight of the game you catch in the trap.

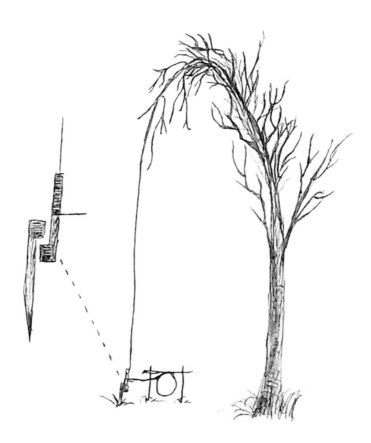

Once you are familiar with spring snares, you can also use them for fishing purposes. The setup of the trap is basically the same, but you substitute the snare loop for a fishing line and hook. Set the trap up along the shoreline and place a baited hook into the water. When a fish takes the bait, it will release the trigger, and the springing back of the sapling will hook the fish.

# 5 MAKING FIRE

One of the most important skills in the outdoors is being able to make fire. In most survival situations it will be a necessity for survival. A fire helps to regulate body temperature, create a light source, boil water for drinking, cook food, make tools, keep unwanted insects and animals at bay, and signal for help.

The ability to make and control fire is one of our most important technical abilities.

# The Fire Triangle

It can be difficult to make fire in a survival situation. That's why it's handy to know the fire triangle.

## SIDE 1:

**Heat or an ignition source.** It might be comforting to know that even the most experienced adventurers will tell you that the best way to start a fire is with a pocket lighter. Knowing how to use bow drills and other friction methods for starting fires is paramount for survival, but a simple lighter is still the best way to create a fire. Nevertheless, this book is about surviving using paracord, so I'll discuss using friction to start fires. Basically, when two objects are rubbed together you get friction, and friction produces heat. The harder and faster the objects are rubbed together, the more heat is produced. Think about when you are cold and you rub your hands together to get warm—same idea!

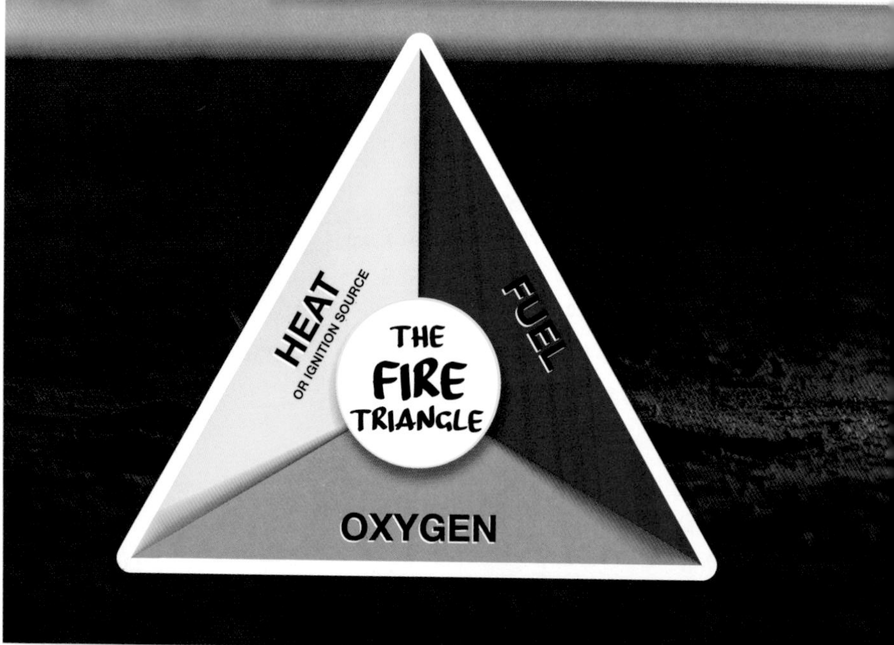

HEAT
OR IGNITION SOURCE

FUEL

THE
**FIRE**
TRIANGLE

**OXYGEN**

## SIDE 2:

**Oxygen.** Obviously there is oxygen all around us. However, there also needs to be proper airflow. If you were to dig a hole and place a fire in it, it will start to burn, but it may die out soon. It would burn much better and longer if a side tunnel could pull air into the fire. When you are roasting marshmallows around a campfire, the fire is pulling air in from the base of the fire while the hot air rises. Controlling airflow is especially important when first starting a fire. Not enough oxygen in the airflow will prevent the ember from staying lit; too much airflow and it will be blown out.

## SIDE 3:

**Fuel.** Even if you have a flame source, a piece of wood doesn't just catch fire when you hold a flame to it. Fuel can be broken down into three smaller categories: tinder, kindling, and fuel. *Tinder* is the driest, finest material that you can find, such as dry grasses, an empty bird's nest, pine needles, etc. Cotton balls and dryer lint make fantastic tinder. *Kindling* includes pieces of wood that should be no thicker than your fingers. Finally, *fuel* is considered to be anything larger than kindling. Start off by igniting the tinder, add some kindling to sustain the flame until a good fire is going, and then add the larger pieces of fuel to sustain it.

## PARA-TIP: Practice Strict Fire Safety

ALWAYS take precautions when starting, maintaining, and extinguishing a fire. When starting and maintaining a fire, make sure that other flammable materials are at a safe distance and that the fire remains contained within a solid, inflammable ring. When you leave an area, always extinguish the fire properly. Pouring water onto a fire is the best way to put it out. Another method is to cover the fire with dirt, but be careful, since the fire can smolder for a long time and even flare back up hours later. Be sure to heed local fire hazard warnings and NEVER leave fires unattended.

## PARA-TIP: Make a Kit

One thing that I always have in my pack is a robust fire-starting kit. There are many different items and materials out there that can go into a kit like this, and the best thing about it is that you can personalize it to what you like to use. My kit includes lighters, matches, ferrocerium rods, magnesium rods, tinder, and fatwood. Fatwood is one of my favorite fire-starting aids, and I highly recommend having some in your pack. Fatwood includes pieces of wood where flammable tree resin has concentrated, making them excellent fire starters. You can take the time to find your own fatwood in the forest or purchase it cheaply by the bag. When I find a big enough piece of it, I like to make a small hole in one end and string a piece of paracord through it. To this, I will also add a ferrocerium rod with a metal scraper. I tie it all together and have a handy paracord lanyard for some of my fire-making tools.

# PROJECT
# PARACORD MATCH

## WHAT YOU WILL NEED

- Small length of paracord
- Pine resin or a type of wax
- Cutting utensil
- Heat source

### Estimated Time for Project

- 20 minutes, mainly waiting for the wax to melt and cool

Candlewicks are made from natural materials such as cotton or jute because they absorb wax and produce a char layer when burned. Paracord is made from nylon, a synthetic material. Trying to use the yarns as a wick doesn't work very well because they don't absorb wax well and they burn very quickly. However, if a whole piece of paracord is immersed and covered in wax, it will burn twice as long as plain paracord. It will also increase the rigidity of the paracord, making it easier to hold in place when it is on fire. This gives it a longer burn time, which in turn gives you more time to get a fire going. The wax-covered piece of paracord in the picture was roughly 6 in. (15 cm) long and burned for about one minute.

**1.** Simply dip a length of paracord into melted wax or resin. Lift it out and allow it to cool. I like to leave some of the yarns exposed because they light faster.

**2.** Once it is cooled, dip it in again and pull it out.

**3.** Repeat this process several times in order to build a layer of wax or resin on the outside of the paracord. Couple this paracord match with a lighter or other flame source to greatly increase your chances of getting a fire going while saving lighter fluid and matches.

# PROJECT
# PARACORD TINDER

## WHAT YOU WILL NEED

- Paracord yarns
- Lighter/matches/ ferrocerium rod

### Estimated Time for Project

- 5 minutes

Good tinder can be hard to come across, depending on the weather and where you are. Luckily, paracord can be used as tinder, with minimal work. Simply break down the paracord into its component parts. The black piece of paracord pictured here was presoaked in wax, which is why there is a white residue on it. This allows for the piece to burn a little bit longer.

**1.** Cut one end off of the cordage and pull out the inner yarns. The yarns can be pulled apart further until they look like wool. Form the yarns into a wooly ball about the size of a walnut shell.

**2.** Cut the outer sheath in half and pull it apart just like the yarns. This creates a lot of surface area for a spark to catch. The nylon burns very quickly, so have as much tinder and kindling as possible ready to go.

## PARA-TIP: The One-Match Scenario

If you only have one match available, here is a method for getting a fire going. Make a good pile of paracord fuzz tinder and place it in a dry spot around any other tinder and kindling that you can find. You also need a decent length of whole paracord, about 6 in. (15 cm). Use the match to light the paracord fuzz and the end of the strand. Holding the strand horizontal will allow it to burn like a candlewick, although it will still burn quickly. This method will give you more time to get a fire going than if only a single match is used.

## PARA-TIP: Leave Small Flames Alone

If there is a small flame, do not blow on it! It can take a lot of work to get to the point of having a flame and you don't want to inadvertently blow it out. Hold tinder or kindling above a flame to grow the fire. Only blow onto a fire if you have a good base of embers to work with.

# Friction Fire

I hope you are ready to use your muscles, because it is time to learn friction fire methods. Finding two sticks and rubbing them together as fast as you can is about as basic as you can get in order to make a fire.

**PROJECT: BOW DRILL (PAGE 147)**

**PROJECT: PUMP DRILL (PAGE 148)**

# PROJECT
# BOW DRILL

## WHAT YOU WILL NEED

- Bow-shaped piece of wood
- Length of paracord
- Piece of indented wood or rock
- Piece of wood for spindle
- Piece of wood for the base board

### Estimated Time for Project

- 20 minutes

There are four parts to making a bow drill: the **board**, **spindle**, **bow**, and **handle**. Ideally the board will be a piece of softwood, the spindle will be a hardwood, and the bow and handle can be any type of wood. The handle only works if it has some kind of indentation in it that the spindle can sit in, otherwise the spindle will be impossible to hold in place. The bow can be a green or a dry piece of wood; what matters is that it can withstand the pressure you exert on it. If everything goes well, the friction between the two pieces of wood will create a smoldering wood dust that an ember can be made from. Transfer this ember to your tinder bundle and breathe life into the fire.

**1.** Tie a piece of paracord to both ends of the bow with a slight amount of slack in the line.

**2.** Whittle the spindle so that it is round at the bottom end and more pointed at the top end. Obtain a handle that you can use to place on top of the pointed end of the spindle, such as a rock, another piece of wood, or a seashell.

**3.** Cut a small hole into the board near the edge so that you can also cut a V notch next to it. This notch helps to provide airflow and to funnel the hot dust into a concentrated pile.

**4.** Wrap the spindle around the cordage of the bow, place the spindle into the board hole, and place the handle on top of the spindle.

**5.** Take a knee and place your foot within inches of where the spindle will be drilling. While applying downward pressure with the handle, pull and push the bow back and forth to turn the spindle. Even after failed attempts to make fire, keep the dust that has already been created, because it makes a good base in successive attempts.

## PROJECT
# PUMP DRILL

## WHAT YOU WILL NEED

- A long piece of wood for the spindle
- Several lengths of paracord
- A piece of wood to act as a weight
- A piece of wood for the crossbar
- A piece of wood for the base

### Estimated Time for Project

- 40 minutes

A pump drill is similar to the bow drill method in that it uses friction to create an ember. While it takes more time to make the pump, it requires less energy to use and has a secondary purpose, which is always a major plus (see Para-Tip below).

### PARA-TIP: More Than Fire

The pump drill can be used for more than just making fire. By adding a pointed, hard stone to the tip of the spindle, this setup can be used to drill holes in other materials such as wood and even rocks.

The pump drill is made up of four components:

- **The shaft or spindle:** A long, smooth, straight piece of wood.
- **The cordage:** Tied to the handle and the shaft.
- **The handle:** When moved up and down, spins the shaft.
- **The flywheel:** Provides stability and downward pressure.

There are no specific dimensions for the components, as the pump drill can be as large or as small as you want it. Solid pieces of wood can be used for the handle and the flywheel but only if a tool is available that can be used to drill holes. Using solid pieces of wood will make the construction sturdier, but drilling holes can be tedious or may not be an option.

In the scenario where holes cannot be drilled, several sticks will need to be tied together for the handle and the flywheel. The sticks for the handle need to have a gap in the middle where the spindle can freely move, whereas the sticks being used for the flywheel need to be tightly bound around the spindle.

The two biggest issues that arise with using the pump drill is that the spindle either gets bound up, meaning that it won't turn, or skips out of the hole in the board. Both of these issues usually have to do with the flywheel. If the spindle is binding up, then the flywheel is most likely too heavy. If the spindle is skipping out of the hole, then the flywheel is most likely too light. In both cases, make adjustments by adding or removing weight. The pump drill takes longer to make than the bow drill setup but requires less energy to operate. As the pump drill spins, the handle moves back up the spindle and rewraps the cord around the spindle.

1. Place the handle at least 12 in. (30 cm) or so below the top of the spindle. I call this its "resting place," where it sits when it is not being used.

2. From here, tie one end of paracord to one end of the handle. Secure it to the top of the spindle by splitting the wood slightly, threading the cord through, and tying off the remaining paracord to the other end of the handle. When it is together, the cord should be taut and form an equilateral triangle with the handle.

3. Once the pump drill is complete, the only other piece you will need is a board. Cut out a notch and a starting hole where the tip of the spindle will be placed.

4. Place the spindle into the hole and hand turn the spindle while holding onto the handle. This will cause the paracord to wrap around the spindle while pulling the handle upward. When the majority of the paracord has been wrapped, the handle can be pressed back down, spinning the spindle. After going down, the handle should go back up the spindle without much resistance and rewrap the paracord. Doing these motions over and over provides a continuous movement that will produce friction and heat between the spindle and the board.

## PROJECT
# FIRE BUNDLE

### WHAT YOU WILL NEED

- One length of paracord
- Several logs

**Estimated Time for Project**

- 5 minutes

The two elements that are the most problematic when trying to start a fire are moisture and wind. There is a very simple way to deal with both of these, and it doesn't require much paracord. By keeping the initial base of the fire up off of the ground, the base isn't resting on the wet ground and isn't pulling in moisture that could dampen the surrounding material. The paracord that is used will be completely sacrificed due to the nature of the project. It is better to let the fire burn than to try to untie the paracord and risk losing the fire.

**1.** Find several logs that can be placed together and stood upright.

**2.** Take a length of yarn or paracord and tie it around the logs so that it is snug but not overly tight. The logs can now be tipped outward so that tinder and kindling can be placed inside.

**3.** Lay a thick layer of tinder in first, and then line the sides with pieces of kindling.

**4.** Using extra tinder and kindling, a fire can now be lit on top of the base layer of tinder. The sides of this structure will help to block any wind that would otherwise put out a flame or ember. The more layers of wood there are on the side, the more protected the inner tinder bundle will be.

# PROJECT
# TORCH

## WHAT YOU WILL NEED

- Several thin, long sticks
- Tinder and kindling
- Several lengths of yarns or paracord
- Cutting tool
- Fire

### Estimated Time for Project

- 10–15 minutes to put it all together once material has been collected

1. Collect tinder and sticks. Lay a bundle of sticks on the ground and decide how long you want the torch to be. Break the sticks to the desired length.

2. Layer the tinder material at the top of the torch. Pile the sticks together in the shape of a torch and use paracord to tie them tightly together. Make three individual wraps around the torch, one at the bottom, one in the middle, and one near the top. By spacing the paracord out this way, the torch will stay together even as the fire burns its way down.

How do you carry fire with you into the darkness? With the right materials, a torch can be used effectively to carry fire from one place to another, signal for help, fish or hunt at night, light up a dark place like a cave, and keep mosquitoes at bay. A torch can last anywhere from a few minutes to much longer. Keep in mind that the denser the wood is, the longer the torch will smolder and burn. This is a very helpful tip to remember when transporting fire for a long distance. To prolong the burn time of a torch, green leaves or wood can be added to the fire portion that will take longer to consume over dry material. These instructions are for a small handheld torch. You can scale up to the torch size you prefer.

# PROJECT
# DRYING OUT

## WHAT YOU WILL NEED

- Paracord
- Fire

### Estimated Time for Project

- Depends on items being dried

No clothespins? No problem! Make your own using paracord—see page 179.

Even if you are not tired or there is still light left in the day, it is important to periodically dry yourself by a fire. Shoes, socks, and any other articles of wet clothing should be removed and placed next to a fire. To avoid getting bacteria or bugs in your drying clothes, hang them next to the fire. The added benefit of this is that it will expose more surface area, allowing your clothes to dry out quicker.

Since you have a fire going and are drying out clothing, you should also dry out any tinder or kindling you picked up along the way. Just like the clothing, tie damp tinder or kindling up and hang them next to the fire. This will make it easier the next time you need to get a fire going.

### PARA-TIP: Plan Future Fire Uses

In survival situations, you have to be thinking ahead as much as possible. Once a fire is started, don't become lazy. There are no guarantees with Mother Nature. Use the fire you have now to:

- Help you start another fire tomorrow

- Make charcloth

- Figure out a way to transport the fire in order to save energy and resources

- Dry out wet tinder that can be carried in your pocket

- Collect the coals for use in filtering water, fire starting, as a substitute for toothpaste, and as an improvised writing utensil

# STRAPS FOR CARRYING WOOD

## WHAT YOU WILL NEED

- **Length of paracord at least 3 ft. (1 m) long**

### Estimated Time for Project

- **A few minutes**

Carrying wood can be a real pain. Carrying logs with itchy bark, or branches that are always poking into you, becomes more irritating by the minute. But as long as you have paracord, you don't have to deal with this.

## Option 1

*1.* Using only paracord, create two loops, one on each end of the paracord.

*2.* Wrap the cordage around the bundle of firewood and thread one of the loops through the other. When pulled, the handle loop will cinch the paracord around the wood, which will allow it to be carried.

## Option 2

*1.* If you want more of a carrying handle, find two pieces of wood that are of similar length and width. Take two equal lengths of paracord and tie the ends to the pieces of wood.

*2.* Lay the cordage and handles out and lay the wood on top of the cordage as it is collected.

*3.* After a nice pile has been made, pick up both handles to carry the wood back to your camp.

## Option 3

*1.* Place the circle of paracord on the ground, then with one hand pinch the top of the circle and with the other hand pinch the opposite side of the circle.

*2.* Pull the two ends away from each other to stretch out the paracord. The wood that is collected should be placed in the middle of the cord so that there is enough paracord sticking out in order to wrap the bundle up.

*3.* Once you have collected enough wood, pull the paracord on both sides of the bundle up and over the top of the wood. Take one side of the cord and pull it under the other side of the cord. When pulled through, this will be the carrying handle.

# 6 HEALTH AND EMERGENCIES

Everyone should be knowledgeable in basic first aid techniques that can help stabilize a person until proper medical attention can be administered. It is usually not the big things that get us, but the accumulation of little things—things like insect bites, a small cut that is ignored and becomes infected, or drinking dirty water and getting sick. In this section you'll learn how to use paracord for basic first aid measures so that little problems don't become big problems.

*The following section is for informational use only and should not be regarded as professional medical advice.*

Use water to stay clean, healthy, and happy.

# PROJECT
# HANDWASHING KIT

## WHAT YOU WILL NEED

- Short lengths of paracord
- Plastic bottle
- Cutting tool

### Estimated Time for Project

- 5 minutes

Sickness can be a death sentence in a survival situation. One of the best ways to avoid becoming ill is by washing your hands as much as possible. It is estimated that a person touches his or her face, on average, several thousand times in a single day. Dirty hands around the mouth, nose, and eyes offer germs an easy way into the body.

Even if soap or another cleaning medium is available, the problem with handwashing is having enough clean water. In a survival situation, clean water is a critical and precious resource. I have seen too many survival TV shows and movies where someone carelessly splashes water everywhere as though they can just refill at the tap. Once clean water is obtained, it has to be properly controlled and taken care of, because you may not know when you can get more.

**1.** Using a knife, cut a small hole in the cap of the bottle. The hole needs to be slightly smaller than the diameter of the paracord; this will create a better seal between the cap and the cordage.

**2.** Cut one end of paracord and use a lighter to burn it to a fine point.

**3.** Thread the pointed end through the hole of the cap until there are several inches (about 10 centimeters) of paracord going into the bottle.

**4.** Now remove the cap and on the pointed end of the paracord tie several overhand knots.

**5.** Replace the cap and pull the paracord on the outside of the bottle so that the knots sit firmly inside the cap.

**6.** When there is clean water in the bottle, the bottle should be inverted so that the paracord is hanging down. The paracord will act like a wick and direct a small amount of water in a controlled manner so that you can wash your hands without wasting too much water.

# PROJECT
## SHOWER IN A BOTTLE

### WHAT YOU WILL NEED

- Plastic water bottle
- Cutting tool
- At least 3 ft. (1 m) of paracord
- Clean water

#### Estimated Time for Project

- A few minutes to make the bottle setup, extra time if warming the water

Like handwashing, bathing is a good way to maintain hygiene, which in turn is a preventative first aid measure. An interesting side effect of maintaining hygiene is the morale boost it gives you. They may seem like small tasks, but going through the steps of handwashing and bathing are ways to take care of ourselves so we feel better overall. Plus, it also gives us a feeling of returning to normal routines, which can be comforting.

For this project, use a regular plastic bottle; usually they are not hard to find, littered as they are throughout the world. The bigger the bottle, the better, because the size will determine how long the shower will run! The one-liter plastic water bottle shown here is probably the most common. By adjusting how tight the cap is screwed on, the water flow can be sped up or slowed down. The shower depicted in the photo (taken during an ice storm) lasted almost three minutes. With the cap fully off, the bottle emptied in just twenty-five seconds.

1. Using a cutting tool, puncture small holes in the bottom of the bottle along the perimeter. These holes should be at the lowest point of the bottle. I recommend making the holes about half the size of a pencil eraser. The size of the holes is really a personal choice, as the size will determine how much and how fast water will come out.

2. Next, find a spot where the bottle can be hung, such as a low tree branch. Throw a length of a paracord over the branch to estimate how much cordage you will need. Tie one end of the paracord around the neck of the bottle with a few simple overhand knots.

3. When it's shower time, simply fill the bottle with clean water, hoist the bottle up into the air, stand under it, and wash up!

**PARA-TIP: Have a Warm Shower Even in the Wild**

There are two ways to warm up water when there isn't a hot tap around. The first is to set full water containers out in the sun and let the sun warm them up. This might take a while. The second is to warm up the water by using fire. Be extremely mindful when using this method so you don't burn yourself with water that is too hot. When the temperature is where you want it, transfer it to the shower bottle and scrub up.

# PROJECT
# PROTECTING YOUR SKIN

## WHAT YOU WILL NEED

- Paracord
- Tree bark section(s)

### Estimated Time for Project

- 10 minutes

In a survival situation, it is always important to protect exposed areas of your body from the hazards of the environment. Even certain tall grasses can make small cuts in the skin that can cause problems if they become infected.

You can make durable skin coverings by strapping tree bark onto yourself using paracord as the straps. Remember, never tie paracord tightly around the body, as it could reduce circulation or irritate your skin.

# PROJECT
# PARACORD STRETCHERS

## WHAT YOU WILL NEED

- Lengths of wood for the frame
- Paracord
- Canvas or tarp
- Knife

### Estimated Time for Project

- Up to an hour

There may come a point where a member of your group becomes ill or cannot walk any more. You will have to evaluate the circumstances to determine if it is better to leave them in a safe place while you continue on for help, or to find some way to bring them with you. When it comes to constructing a stretcher, you have a few options.

### Option 1: Basic Stretcher

One of the simplest stretchers that you can make consists of two sturdy branches, a canvas or tarp, and some paracord. Two crossbeams of wood can be attached, one on each end, to prevent the stretcher from folding in on itself too much.

1. Lay the tarp flat out onto the ground.

2. Next, take the branches and place them on the top edges of the tarp.

3. Begin rolling the branches with the tarp until there is a little over 24 in. (61 cm) of tarp left in the middle for a person to be placed (this will need to be adjusted depending on the width of the patient). There will also need to be enough of the branches sticking out past the tarp so that these sections can be used as handles for carrying the injured or sick person.

**4.** Use whole pieces of paracord to secure the tarp to the branches. Holes may need to be cut through the tarp in order to accomplish this. It takes two people to carry the stretcher.

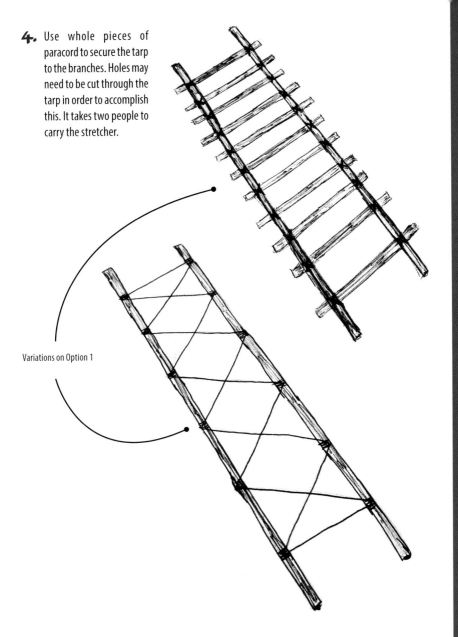

Variations on Option 1

## Option 2: Sled

You can also fashion a sled pulled by one or more people using paracord. You need something big and strong enough to support a person. Tie paracord on one end of the sled platform so that it can be pulled. It can be difficult to pull such a sled across rocky or rugged terrain.

## Option 3: Travois

This structure is typically used more for carrying supplies but can be used as a stretcher. The traditional name for this is a *travois*. It is basically a large A-frame of wood with crossbeams. You will need at least one crossbeam toward the bottom, but you can add as many as needed. The top of the A-frame pictured is the front of the stretcher where it is pulled. When it is laid down on the ground, you will stand in between the V. The sides of the V can be used as handles to pick the frame up and pull it.

 **PARA-TIP: Drag Your Gear**

The stretchers described are not just for carrying people. Take some weight off your back by using one of them to drag supplies behind you on the trail.

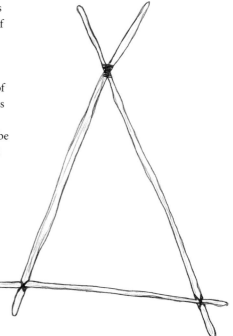

# PROJECT
# PARACORD SUTURES

## WHAT YOU WILL NEED

- Needle
- 3 ft. (1 m) of paracord yarns
- Scissors or knife

### Estimated Time for Project

- 5–10 minutes

I have to say up front that I have never personally used paracord for sutures, but I have heard that it is a viable material for the job. Please do your own extensive research when it comes to the type of wounds that require suturing and how to properly do so. Paracord sutures will need to be removed at some point as they will not break down like modern suture materials do. It is extremely important that all of the materials being used for sutures be sterilized as best you can before being used (see page 169).

This project relies on the "continuous suture" method. It's one of the easiest, especially one-handed. I use a rather large needle and a whole yarn piece in the pictures, just so you can see the method better. A smaller needle (curved if you have one) is better, as is breaking the paracord yarn down into a finer strand. If you have a pair of pliers available, I highly recommend using them to insert and pull the needle through the skin.

As with everything in this book, practice, practice, practice! I think it's safe to say that most people have never had to suture a wound. There are a number of ways in which you can practice this skill at home. Small plastic or foam dummies are available for purchase that are specifically made for this. I have never used these but have heard good things about them. Or you could be like me, and use a piece of raw meat from your refrigerator. Regardless of where you find your "patient," practice suturing with both hands but also using only one hand—in a survival situation, you may have to suture yourself.

**1.** Cut a strand of yarn to use for the suturing thread. Several feet (about a meter) should be sufficient. Thread the yarn through the needle eye and tie it off with several overhand knots. Push the needle through the skin on one side of the cut, into the cut, and through the skin on the other side.

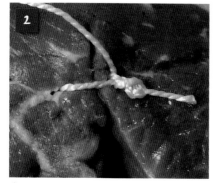

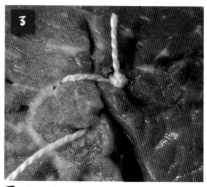

**2.** Start the needle just below one end of the cut so that when the first loop is pulled taut, it closes the end gap. Once you have pulled the needle and the majority of the yarn through, secure the end by tying what is called a surgeon's knot. With the long end of the yarn, make several loops and pull the cut end through. Add a couple of simple overhand knots (probably not a perfect surgeon's knot, but very close). When the first knot is completed, go ahead and cut off the excess.

**3.** It may be necessary to keep slight pressure on the thread so that previous loops don't come undone. Begin your line of sutures, starting on the side that knot is closest to. In this case it is the right side. Push the needle in through the right side and out of the left side. Make your lines at a slight angle instead of straight across, as this seems to hold everything together better.

## PARA-TIP: Stitch Depth

I don't have any measurements to give you in terms of how far down to thread the needle through the skin. If it is too high up and superficial, then the sutures won't hold and can be torn out. If it is threaded too deep, then it is going to be very painful and can cause more damage. Before attempting any first aid treatments, always consult a medical professional if possible.

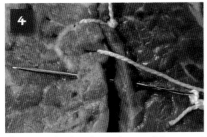

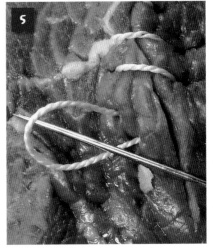

**4.** Bring the thread over the top of the cut and insert the needle on the right side and out through the left. Bring the yarn taut to pull the top layer of the cut together. Continue this step all along the length of the laceration until you get to the end. Note: You definitely don't want the knot on the needle eye as large as the one in the picture. That would be rather uncomfortable when it is pulled through the skin.

**5.** As is the case with many cordage projects, there are a number of ways to end this suture line. Here's how to end it if you only have one hand available. Instead of bringing the yarn over the top and pushing the needle through the right side, insert the needle through the left side and out the right side. I do not pull this line tight but instead leave enough slack so that a loop can be made.

**6.** Pass the needle through the loop several times and pull it tight. Cut off the excess.

## ARM SLING

Trying to immobilize an arm when you only have one good arm can be tricky. Luckily, a simple sling can be made out of just a few feet (a meter) of paracord. Paracord around the open skin can be uncomfortable and rub the skin raw. Use any extra clothing material available, like a sock or bandanna, to pad the area between the paracord and the skin.

**1.** Get a rough estimate of how much cord you will need by placing your arm where you want it to rest against your body. Loosely wrap one end of the paracord around your arm, then stretch it up and around the back of your neck and back down to your arm.

**2.** On both ends of the cord, make a non-adjustable loop that is large enough to fit your arm through. The loops should not be adjustable because otherwise they can tighten around your arm, which can cause further problems.

**3.** Slide your arm through the first loop and push the loop up toward the elbow.

**4.** Take the paracord and wrap it up and behind your neck and back down. Slide your arm through the second loop, which should be near your wrist.

## WOOD SPLINTS

If you can, find pieces of wood that are the length of the area that needs to be splinted. Generally you will only need two pieces of wood to splint a finger, arm, or leg.

**1.** Place a piece of wood on either side of the area that needs to be immobilized.

**2.** Wrap paracord around the wood splints in order to keep them in place. Do not wrap the cord too tightly

**3.** Knot everything together.

# CORDAGE SPLINTS

## WHAT YOU WILL NEED

- 3 ft. (1 m) of paracord

### Estimated Time for Project

- A few minutes

Sometimes making splints out of wood can be difficult, especially if you need to immobilize fingers on one hand or you can't find materials. An easy way to get around this is to simply wrap the affected fingers with paracord. You want the wrap to be snug in order to prevent movement, but not tight, otherwise you will reduce circulation to those fingers. Use whole paracord rather than the yarns.

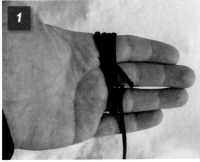

**1.** Make the wraps snug so that they stay in place but not so tight that your fingers begin to turn purple. In this example, I used 5 ft. (1.5 m) of whole paracord to wrap my index and middle fingers. Start by placing one end of the paracord parallel between the fingers, and begin wrapping the rest of the cord around to keep this end in place.

**2.** To finish, leave the last few wraps loose so you can thread the end of the paracord underneath them toward the base of the fingers. After the end has been threaded through, pull it to tighten up the rest of it. This isn't a permanent fix, and the paracord can slide off the ends of your fingers if there is too much movement in your hands, but it works well in a pinch.

PROJECT

# PARACORD TOURNIQUET

## WHAT YOU WILL NEED

- Length of paracord
- A stick

### Estimated Time for Project

- A few minutes

### PARA-TIP: Only Use This in Extreme Situations

**Caution!** Paracord, by itself, is not an ideal material for a tourniquet. It can apply a lot of pressure to a small area, which can cause further damage to skin and tissue. Using paracord or other small diameter pieces of cordage as a tourniquet should only be used as a short-term solution or if there is no other option available. One way around this is by looping the paracord back on itself many times to create a thicker rope with more surface area.

The purpose of a tourniquet is to slow or stop the bleeding of a major wound until proper medical care can be administered. A tourniquet should be placed above the wound site in order to accomplish this. Tourniquets are usually applied to areas of the body where a limb has sustained damage (e.g., an arm or leg). For this project, I use a long length, roughly 10 ft. (3 m), and fold it in half a few times so that on one end there are loops. By folding the paracord several times you get more surface area, which reduces the chance of inflicting further damage, unlike using a single piece of paracord.

**1.** Wrap the paracord around your upper thigh (or wherever you are addressing a wound) and thread the cut ends through the loop and pull tight.

**2.** Twist the strap to reduce downstream blood flow to the wound. To help twist and apply the proper amount of tension on the site, wrap the end of the paracord around a small piece of wood that can be used as a handle.

## TREATING BLISTERS

Blisters can be a real pain to deal with, especially when they are located on hands and feet. While I don't have any personal experience with the treatment described here, I have heard of it being successful.

**1.** First poke a small hole in the side of the blister to allow drainage. This alleviates the pressure and pain so that you can go about your work.

**2.** You can stick a paracord yarn (not whole paracord) into the hole to help wick moisture away from the blister, which helps speed up the healing process.

## STERILIZING EQUIPMENT

One of the most important aspects of proper first aid is making sure the tools and materials being used are sterile. This can become a problem in a survival situation where supplies are limited and often have to be reused. Paracord cannot be used to sterilize items directly, but by using the projects in this book to make fire and get clean water, we can come close to cleaning dirty supplies.

The best way to sterilize instruments is by boiling water in a container large enough to hold the dirty items. Boiling dirty bandages, for example, is a good way of killing off any bacteria hiding away in the fabric. A clean piece of paracord can then be used to hang the instruments up to dry, away from any sources of contamination. When the bandage is clean, fold it up and tuck it away in the cleanest place you have. Ideally this boiling method should be applied to any first aid tools prior to use, especially ones that go beyond skin level. A needle being used for stitches, for example, should be sterilized with a flame or boiled.

# 7 CAMPSITES AND COOKING

**A**fter a long day of walking, hunting, or fishing, setting up camp can seem like an exhausting chore. Making a shelter, protecting resources and food, cooking, making tools—the list can go on and on. Having paracord on hand makes some of these tasks possible or easier.

Just because it's the wilderness doesn't mean it has to be uncomfortable.

## PROJECT
# HANGING UP YOUR FOOD

### WHAT YOU WILL NEED

- Length of paracord
- Weight, such as a rock or piece of wood

**Estimated Time for Project**

- 5 minutes

In a survival situation, food and clean water can be difficult things to come across. It's heartbreaking to wake up in the morning to find your food pilfered by animals in the night. That is why it's a good idea to hang up your food when you are sleeping or venturing away from camp for any amount of time.

**1.** Take a good length of cordage and tie a weight on one end, such as a rock, monkey fist (see page 100), or chunk of wood. On the opposite end of the cordage, secure your food source or pack.

**2.** Now find a suitable tree branch that the food can be hung from. While standing on the ground it can be hard to tell how solid a branch will be. Be careful when hoisting items up, and be prepared for falling limbs. When hanging up food, it should be 10 ft. (3 m) away from the trunk of the tree and 20 ft. (6 m) off the ground.

**3.** With all your might, throw the weighted end of the paracord over the branch and pull the food up. Let the food hang 1 ft. (30 cm) or so below the branch so climbers won't be able to reach it.

**4.** Tie off the weighted end of the cordage so the food pack remains suspended. Heavy packs can sometimes be difficult to hoist up. Using a metal shackle (like those from a paracord bracelet) as an improvised pulley can make this task easier.

PROJECT
# CAMP CHAIR

## WHAT YOU WILL NEED

- At least 4 pieces of wood
- A tarp
- Paracord

### Estimated Time for Project

- 30 minutes

**1.** Take three branches and tie the ends together to create a lopsided A-frame.

**2.** Take a smaller branch and tie it between two of the frame pieces; this will be where your bottom will rest.

**3.** String a piece of material, such as a tarp, between the two side posts of the chair so that you can lean back in it comfortably. The fishing net project (see page 124) works as a great substitute.

When it comes to taking a seat in the wild, usually the hard ground is less than ideal, and a log isn't much better. If you find yourself in an area where you might have to spend some time, you'll want to construct a simple chair in which to rest your weary legs. This chair doesn't take a lot of time to make and can be much more comfortable than the ground or a log. For this project you will need a minimum of four pieces of wood to use for the frame of the chair and ideally a small tarp or some other material for the backrest of the chair.

# PROJECT
# PARACORD BED

## WHAT YOU WILL NEED

- Wood
- Trees
- Paracord
- A tarp or canvas if available

### Estimated Time for Project

- 1 hour

A bed raised off the ground is simple to construct and can help keep you out of reach of creepy crawlies at night, as well as safely off the cold, wet ground, which can suck a lot of heat from your body. There are different ways to make a paracord bed.

**Option 1.** The first option is to set the bed up between two trees, using them as part of the framework. Place two sturdy branches horizontal between the two tree trunks and secure them with paracord. Next, attach a tarp or other pieces of wood as crossbeams between the two horizontal pieces.

**Option 2.** This setup can be accomplished without the use of trees. You will need to incorporate four pieces of wood or other natural materials to act as anchor points. Secure branches along these anchor points to finish the frame. Tie or lay other pieces of wood across the frame in which to lie down on. However, if you really want to be comfortable, I suggest putting down a layer of pine boughs to create a natural mattress.

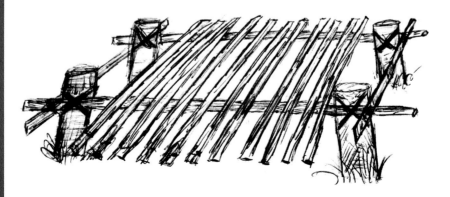

# PROJECT
# SECURITY PERIMETER

## WHAT YOU WILL NEED

- Containers that will make sound
- Paracord

### Estimated Time for Project

- 15 minutes

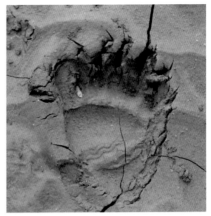

Set up your security system before you go to bed so you don't wake up to this in your campsite.

When you are bedding down for the night, the last thing that you want to worry about is an unwanted guest entering your camp. Having some way of alerting you to an intruder's presence can be a lifesaving security measure.

**1.** Take a long length of paracord and tie each end to some anchor point, such as a tree. The paracord should be tied about 1 ft. (30 cm) off the ground.

**2.** Use this line to hang any items that you can find that will make noise when they strike each other. These items can be soda cans, soup cans, pieces from your mess kit, and even some rocks will make a loud enough sound for you to hear. When an intruder comes along and trips over the main line, it will bounce the hanging items and they should bang together. The sound of this primitive security system should give you enough time to prepare for something entering the campsite. Do your best to remember where the line is so you don't trip over it yourself!

# Shelters

One of the first things you need to do when you find a camp location is to set up a shelter. Shelters do not have to be elaborate structures, especially if you do not plan on spending a lot of time in one location. A shelter really only needs to be large enough so that you can lay down somewhat comfortably in it and get a break from the elements. A simple tarp shelter can offer enough protection from the elements to get you through the night. There are several different ways in which tarps and natural materials can be set up for shelters.

**PROJECT: TARP SHELTERS (PAGE 177)**

**PROJECT: LEAN-TO (PAGE 178)**

**PROJECT: TEEPEE TARP SHELTER (PAGE 179)**

**PROJECT: WALLS AND HEAT REFLECTOR PAGE 180)**

# PROJECT
# TARP SHELTERS

## WHAT YOU WILL NEED

- Canvas or plastic tarp
- Several lengths of paracord
- Sticks to be used as stakes
- Rocks or similar to weigh down the edges (optional)

### Estimated Time for Project

- Varies on the shelter, 15–20 minutes

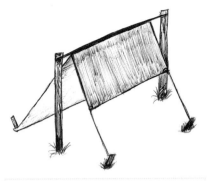

There are a couple options for tarp shelters. What you choose will depend on the size of your tarp and other resources. Set up the poles and paracord line between the poles first, then choose an option.

## PARA-TIP: Working with Tarps without Eyelets

You may have a piece of material that you are going to use as a tarp but that doesn't have any of the metal ring eyelets in which to tie the paracord. If you find yourself in that situation, here is a little trick. Find a small rock or other object that you can place near the corner of the material. When the material is wrapped around the rock, it creates what I call a little "button." Paracord can now be tied around this button in order to hold the material up.

**Option 1.** Always place the largest wall of a shelter on the windward side; that is to say, the direction in which the wind is blowing. This will offer the most protection against the weather. Make your shelter with the steepest wall possible so that rain or snow slides off easily.

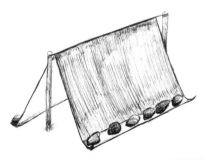

**Option 2.** Instead of using stakes and additional cordage, rocks or logs can be used to weigh down the edges of a tarp. Just be careful that any jagged edges don't tear holes in the material.

# PROJECT
# LEAN-TO

## WHAT YOU WILL NEED

- Paracord
- Branches, vegetation

### Estimated Time for Project

- 30 minutes

A lean-to is probably one of the easiest shelters you can construct. It consists of natural materials leaning against a crossbeam. You can make one without paracord, but using paracord will give you more control.

**1.** Find a spot between two trees or structures where you can suspend a crossbeam. This can also be accomplished by using a large downed tree to lean branches against. Make sure that the branch you are using for the crossbeam is long enough that the ends stick beyond the trunks of the two trees. This will allow you to secure the crossbeam with paracord around the tree trunk.

**2.** Gather branches and other pieces of wood that can be leaned up against the crossbeam. This will provide a wall that shields against the elements. Other vegetation like grasses or pine boughs can be layered on top of this wall to shore up any gaps and provide even more protection. Vegetation should be stacked from the bottom to the top, overlapping the previous layer. When done correctly, rain will run down the lean-to wall like the roof shingles of a house.

# TEEPEE TARP SHELTER

## WHAT YOU WILL NEED

- Paracord
- Tarp
- Anchors

### Estimated Time for Project

- 30 minutes

If you have a piece of waterproof material such as a large tarp, this type of shelter can be easily made. The one requirement is that there is an overhanging anchor point, like a tree branch. This is a quick way of setting up a shelter in a pinch.

**1.** Lay the tarp out and find the center of the material. Place a rock or other small object in the center and pull the tarp up around the object. This provides a point where the paracord can be attached to the tarp.

**2.** Take the opposite end of the paracord and heave it over the overhanging branch. Pull the paracord so that the tarp begins to lift up off of the ground.

**3.** Tie the end of the paracord to an anchor point. Pull the edges of the tarp outward and stake them down. Stones or pieces of wood can be used as improvised stakes by placing them on top of the edges. Leave one area of the edge unstaked so that you can crawl in.

## CLOTHESPIN

A clothespin may come in handy when trying to hold two things together. These are quite easy to make and more useful than you might think. You can make a larger version of this clothespin to use as a bushcraft vise for holding something still while you work on it.

**1.** Take a piece of wood and split it down the center, roughly halfway to three-quarters of the way down.

**2.** For a small clothespin, use a paracord yarn and wrap it around the piece of wood. This will provide tension on the open end of the wood and help to prevent the wood from splitting all the way through.

# PROJECT
# WALLS AND HEAT REFLECTOR

## WHAT YOU WILL NEED

- **Thick branches**
- **Long logs**
- **Cutting tool**
- **Paracord**

### Estimated Time for Project

- **Depends on the size of the wall being made, but a small 4 × 4 ft. (1.2 m × 1.2 m) section could be made in 30 minutes or less**

reference. This branch can now be used as a measuring stick.

By constructing continuous sections end to end, a security wall can be built around your camp. To use this as a heat reflector, choose a spot that is close to your shelter and fire. Place the wall about 1–2 ft. (30–61 cm) away from the fire so that it doesn't burn. The wall helps to "bounce" the surrounding heat back toward the shelter, instead of it being lost.

The steps in this project are going to be used to build one thing that can have two different functions. By using a little bit of paracord and some wood, you can build a wall that can be used to keep animals out, block wind, and serve as a heat reflector for your fire. The basic wall consists of three parts:

- **Wooden poles:** you will need four for each section
- **Branches or logs:** for the horizontal body of the wall
- **Paracord:** to help keep it all together

The height and length of the wall is going to depend on the materials and tools available to you. Wall sections that are roughly 4 ft. by 4 ft. (1.2 m by 1.2 m) are best. Use measurements based on lengths that are familiar to you. For example, if you grab a branch and stand it upright, then you can use your height as a

1. Find four sturdy branches that can be used as the poles. On one end of each of the poles, use a knife to carve a spear point.

2. Pound two of the poles into the ground, spear point down, leaving enough width between them so that logs or branches can be stacked.

3. Place the other two poles directly across from the first two poles. The benefit of having a hatchet is that the backside of the head can be used as a hammer for this step. If you don't have one, use a "bush hammer," which is just another piece of wood.

4. Now the space between the poles can be filled in by lying logs or branches horizontally, stacking them from the ground up. Stop stacking the wood a few inches (about 10 centimeters) from the tops of the poles. You could stop here, but it's better to use a length of paracord to wrap the top sections of the poles together on each side of the wall for additional stability.

**PARA-TIP: Mortar Gaps with Mud**

Because you can't always run to the local hardware store for perfectly straight lumber, there will most certainly be gaps in the walls. These are easily fixed by filling them with any natural material. Smaller branches can be woven in or grasses and mud can be applied like brick mortar.

# Cooking with Paracord

The simple things in life often provide the most pleasure. A warm meal and cold drink around a fire is among the most enjoyable and comforting. Another obvious benefit of campfire cooking is killing any bacteria the food harbors.

Since paracord is made out of nylon, it will melt and burn when subjected to enough heat. However, it can be used in conjunction with other materials to aid in cooking.

**PROJECT: PREPPING MEAT (PAGE 183)**

**PROJECT: BOILING WATER IN A PLASTIC CONTAINER (PAGE 184)**

**PROJECT: SMOKING MEAT (PAGE 186)**

# PROJECT
# PREPPING MEAT

One way of saving the edge on a cutting tool is by using paracord yarns to **cut and process food**. Have you ever seen fancy cheese makers cutting cheese? They sometimes use a piece of string to cut through a block of cheese. A paracord yarn can be used to do the same.

Paracord yarn can also help in **skinning fish** or other game. To descale a fish, place the fish on a flat surface. Take a length of yarn and put the midsection of yarn at the tail end of the fish. Pull the yarn down and toward the head of the fish so that the yarn catches the scales, which will make them easier to remove. It may be necessary to hold onto the fish's tail or to tack it down with a temporary stake.

For **skinning other animals**, cut a line along the hide where the yarn can be placed under it. Hold one end of the yarn in each hand and work the yarn in a back-and-forth motion to cut through the connective tissue.

In some instances, you may have trouble producing enough pressure for the yarn to **cut through meat**. There is a trick that you can use in order to produce a lot more cutting pressure. Grab a small piece of wood and wrap the yarn around it so there is a loop hanging down. Place the item you wish to cut on the inside of

## WHAT YOU WILL NEED

- A paracord yarn
- A small piece of wood

### Estimated Time for Project

- A few minutes

this loop. Now, using the wood as a handle, begin twisting the yarn in one direction over and over. As the yarn is twisted it will tighten and exert more and more pressure, slowly cutting its way through meat. This little tool can cut through other materials, too.

# PROJECT
# BOILING WATER IN A PLASTIC CONTAINER

There is going to come a time when the water you collect will need to be boiled, but a metal container may not be available. Did you know that you can boil water in a plastic water bottle?

Boiling water in a plastic container works when we understand the temperatures involved. Water boils at a temperature of 212° Fahrenheit (100° Celsius). Most plastics can withstand temperatures above this. If the plastic bottle is subjected to low, consistent heat, you can bring the water to a boil before the container melts.

**Caution!** Boiling water with this method should only be done as a last-ditch effort if you cannot find any other suitable containers. The heat applied to the plastic releases harmful chemicals that leech into the water.

## WHAT YOU WILL NEED

- A plastic container
- Paracord
- Fire

### Estimated Time for Project

- 20 minutes

1. First, get a fire going and fill up a bottle with water. Leave the cap off the container so that pressure doesn't build up when the water is heated. Next, tie a length of paracord around the neck of the bottle with a few overhand knots. Tie the other end of the cord to an anchor point above the fire—a tree branch, tripod, or a stick that you are holding. Find a spot where the flames barely lick the bottom of the bottle. Monitor the fire closely and adjust the height of the bottle so that the plastic doesn't become too hot and melt.

2. The top of the bottle will deform from the heat, but that is to be expected. You will know that the bottle is close enough to the heat when bubbles begin to form on the sides. The standard time for boiling water for drinking purposes is one minute at a rolling boil. This changes slightly with altitude, so boiling for three minutes is sufficient for most locations.

## PROJECT
# SMOKING MEAT

Smoking meat is a means of preserving it for several days or longer without refrigeration. Given time, the lower temperature of smoke will dry out the food. This greatly decreases the water content and thereby starves bacteria of the ability to ruin the food. Smoking meat can take a long time, but cutting the meat a certain way will speed up the process.

**1.** Cut the meat into thin slices so there is more surface area exposed for the smoke to dry. An alternative is to cut slots into the meat. The slots should be cut at an angle so that when the meat is hung they will fall open, exposing more of the meat to the smoke. This allows the meat to remain in one piece for easier transport.

**2.** Once the meat has been properly cut, it is time to hang it up. Small holes can be cut into the thin slices, and they can be strung onto paracord between two wood posts like a popcorn necklace. A sharpened stick can also be used by poking it through the meat, then hanging the stick from a tree branch above the fire.

**3.** Hang the meat close enough to the fire so most of the smoke is passing over the meat. If the meat begins to sizzle, then it is too close to the heat and should be moved farther away. When the meat becomes brittle and has the consistency of jerky, it is done. This meat can now be carried for several days and still be edible. Soaking the dried meat in a bit of clean water for a few minutes will make it easier to chew.

### PARA-TIP: Don't Discard Bad Meat

If the dried meat begins to smell rancid or you suspect that it has gone bad, do not eat it. However, don't throw it away either. Instead, hold onto it and use it for fish bait or to lure other animals. Just be sure to keep it separate from your good food.

## PARA-TIP: Supporting Cookware

Normally when I want to support a pot or some other container above a fire, I like to do so with a forked branch. If there is already a structure over the fire, you can simply hang a pot by its handles by supporting it with a length of paracord. (This can save you time by not having to look for the right kind of branches). Instead of tying the paracord to the branch above, throw it over and tie one end to a rock or log. This will create a pulley-like system so that you can raise or lower the pot in order to regulate temperature.

## HANGING GRILL

Depending on what materials and supplies are available, it may be easier and quicker to make a hanging grill above your fire than to build a traditional tripod. Two separate pieces of paracord will be needed.

**1.** Hang the two pieces of cord above the fire and to the side in such a way that they are hanging loops. Make sure that the paracord is far enough from the fire that it does not melt.

**2.** Span the branches across the fire so that their ends are resting in the loops. When you are finished, it will look like you have made a bridge. This can be used to slowly heat containers or to hang meat from the individual sticks.

# 8 MAKING AND MODIFYING TOOLS

Survival situations can happen in the blink of an eye. They are thrust upon us whether we like it or not. In order get through the experience, we need to adapt and solve problems. Have you ever heard the saying, "It is better to have something and not need it than to need something and not have it"? In this section we'll learn how to protect the gear you do have and make tools that can help you survive.

Knowing how to manufacture helpful items will give you peace of mind.

# PROJECT
# REPAIRING AN AX HANDLE

## WHAT YOU WILL NEED

- Ax head
- Piece of wood for the handle
- Paracord
- Cutting utensil

### Estimated Time for Project

- 15 minutes

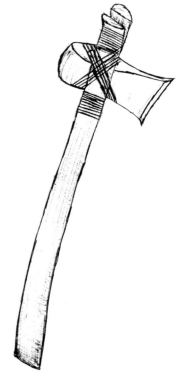

The extra weight an ax adds to a pack is acceptable when you consider the variety of functions it has. But what if you need to fix its handle? Here is a simple, fairly quick method for making an ax handle.

**1.** Find a tree branch that is a couple of inches (a few centimeters) in diameter. Use the ax head or a knife to split the branch down the middle. The wood only needs to be split far enough down so that there is around 3 in. (7.6 cm) sticking above the ax head when it is placed inside.

**2.** Place the ax head in between the split wood. The cordage can now be used to hold the ax head in place. First wrap the paracord around the branch for the first few inches (about 10 centimeters) below the ax head. By doing this first you don't have to worry too much about the wood splitting more than you want it to.

**3.** Wrap the paracord around the branch above the ax head. This pulls the two pieces of wood together, clamping down on the head.

**4.** To finish, wrap the paracord around the branch and the ax head in the shape of an X.

**PARA-TIP: Make a Wild Ax**

You don't have to have a modern ax head in order to have an ax. There are certain rocks that can be used as ax heads by using other rocks to hammer them into shape.

**PARA-TIP: Swing with Caution**

After completing this project, it's a good idea to start out swinging this ax slowly and with a lot of caution. The ax head might not be seated as tightly as you think, so this testing period will give you an opportunity to make adjustments.

Here is an alternative method for an ax head with an eye:

1. Using a cutting tool, shave down the end of a piece of wood so that it fits snugly and has to be pounded into the eye of the metal head.

2. Allow the wood to come through the eye roughly 2 in. (5 cm).

3. Tightly wrap paracord around the handle and ax handle much like in the previous method, around the handle, over the metal head, and around the wood coming through the eye.

# PROJECT
# MAKING A KNIFE

## WHAT YOU WILL NEED

- Bone or rock
- Wood for the handle
- Paracord

### Estimated Time for Project

- Varies depending on the material being used for the blade

The first knife blades were made from pieces of bone or certain kinds of rocks. Some of the cutting edges were as sharp or sharper than surgical scalpels! This project is a good example of why you should always keep your eyes open for resources. The right kind of bone, antler, or rock could be transformed into an invaluable tool.

**1.** When you find the right material for the knife blade, use other rock surfaces to shape and hone the edge. The blade can then be wedged in between wood or similar materials and tied together with paracord.

**2.** Cut out two small notches near where the knife and handle meet. Cordage can then be tied around these notches to keep the connection even tighter.

**3.** If the piece of bone or rock is large enough and shaped correctly, you could simply wrap paracord around the base of it for a handle. It is always important to have some kind of handle so that your hand doesn't slip forward to the sharp blade.

# PROJECT
# TOOL LOOP

## WHAT YOU WILL NEED

- About 18 in. (46 cm) of paracord

### Estimated Time for Project

- A few minutes that can save you hours!

Taking just a few minutes and a little bit of paracord, you can make a loop on the end of most tools. This loop will help you hang onto your most important items—your tools for survival—in the field.

1. A lot of outdoor tools have a hole near the bottom of the handle. Thread one end of paracord through this hole and secure the two cut ends together.

2. This will create one large loop that can be twisted into a smaller loop around the wrist. If you lose your grip on the handle, you won't lose the tool.

# PROJECT
# KNIFE HANDLE

In this project, we are using paracord to add a better grip and some cushion to an uncomfortable handle. You can add this to any tool handle, not just knives. Unless the handle curves or widens at some point at the bottom, though, the wrap can slide off during use.

## WHAT YOU WILL NEED

- Paracord (the length of cord needed depends on how large the tool handle is)
- Cutting tool
- Lighter

### Estimated Time for Project

- 5–10 minutes

Some knife designs like this skinning/gutting knife don't come with scales (handles). Wrapping some paracord around it will make it more comfortable to hold and give it a bit of grip.

**1.** Place one end of paracord at the bottom of the handle so that 1–2 in. (2.5–5 cm) is sticking out. Hold this in place and create a loop that goes up the handle and back down to the bottom.

**2.** Make sure not to wrap paracord over the cut end on the left side of the handle. Bring the two side pieces of the loop close together and, with the working end of the paracord, begin wrapping around the handle starting at the bottom and working your way up.

**4.** While doing this, sometimes you have to keep pushing the wraps down in order to keep them tight and in line. Once the wrap gets to the top of the handle, don't bury the top of the loop under the paracord. There needs to be small bit of it exposed. After the last wrap around the handle, thread the working end of the paracord through the loop.

**3.** It is important that the first turn around the handle is quite tight in order to hold the base of the loop in place. As the wrap progresses upward, be sure to keep the loop as centered as possible and don't let it slide off and around the handle.

**7.** When everything is done, you should end up with a handle wrap that looks like this. It's not a permanent handle, but it is a good temporary solution.

**5.** There doesn't need to be much paracord left on the working end after being threaded through the loop. About 1–2 in. (2–5 cm) should be more than enough. While using one hand to hold the top loose wraps in place, pull on the cut end of cord that is at the bottom of the handle. This will tighten the top loop and cinch down the paracord that was threaded through it. Give it a couple of good tugs to bring the loop down and under the handle wraps.

**6.** The end of paracord sticking out of the bottom can be difficult to pull if the wraps are very tight or if there a lot of them. You may want to use a pair of pliers in order to pull that piece down. When it all feels tight and like it is holding itself in place, cut all of the ends and melt them with a lighter.

# PROJECT
# GRAPPLING HOOK

## WHAT YOU WILL NEED

- Several pieces of thick wood
- Paracord
- Cutting tool

### Estimated Time for Project

- 30 minutes

A grappling hook can be useful in many ways. For instance, it can be used as a climbing aid when ascending or descending steep inclines, it can be thrown from a boat to pull yourself to shore, it can be used as a boat anchor, and it can be used to retrieve fallen items. Depending on how much work you want to put into it, a grappling hook can have as many or as few hooks as you want. This project has three hooks, which gives it a good overall balance.

### PARA-TIP: Don't Go Rock Climbing with This Equipment

Never put your full body weight on any bush-made grappling hook. You don't want to risk it breaking on you.

**1.** To minimize the amount of cutting needed, it will help to find three sections of wood that have forks in them or have a Y shape to them. Give the Y branch a good tug to test its sturdiness; if it doesn't bend or has a slight bend to it, then it will be good to use.

**2.** Tie the pieces of wood around a central post. Use the end of the post for tying on the main section of paracord.

**3.** To tie the main paracord to the end of the central post, drill a hole through the end of the center post in which to thread the paracord through. To make the hole, use the tip of your cutting tool to carve and dig in a circular motion. Then drill about halfway through and start drilling on the other side until the two holes meet. By drilling in this way, it helps to keep the size of the hole smaller, which in turn keeps this anchor point strong.

# PROJECT
# WOOD LADDER

This type of wood ladder consists of wooden rungs that are tied in between two long lengths of paracord. The lengths of paracord that you will need will depend on the length of the ladder that you need.

## WHAT YOU WILL NEED

- **Thick branches**
- **Two long lengths of paracord**

### Estimated Time for Project

- **One hour, but depends on size**

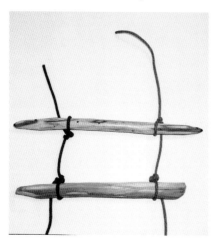

**1.** Tie a manharness hitch (nonadjustable loops along the lengths of the paracord). Make sure that the loops on either side of the paracord are as even as possible.

**2.** Insert the branches into the loops and adjust the paracord to make sure the loops are tight around the wood. Making the wood rungs as even as possible provides for a more stable foothold when climbing up or down.

### PARA-TIP: The Stretcher Design Alternative

An alternative way to make a wood ladder is to make the two-person stretcher (see page 160). This may be a better option when only short pieces of paracord are available. A solid wood ladder/stretcher could also be used as a bridge in certain situations, but use extreme caution when doing so.

# ROPE LADDER

## WHAT YOU WILL NEED

- Paracord (more is better)

**Estimated Time for Project**

- 30 minutes, but depends on size

You may not have the time to spend, or the materials needed, to make a wood ladder. In that case, this variation of a rope ladder is simple and quick to make. The only material you need is paracord itself—how much depends on how far you want to climb. I recommend using as many lengths as possible, to increase the ladder's strength by doubling the cordage onto itself.

*1.* Make nonadjustable loops along the length of the paracord by tying the manharness hitch. The loops need to be large enough to accommodate your hands and feet.

*2.* Secure the top of the rope to an anchor point and use the loops to climb up and down. Since this uses only one length of cord, be aware that the rope will feel unstable. You will twist and turn as you climb.

### PARA-TIP: Make a Tree-Climbing Foot Strap

Make two nonadjustable loops that your foot can slip into. The distance between the loops should be several feet (about a meter), depending on the diameter of the tree. Once the loops are secured around your footwear, you can jump onto the tree trunk, wrapping your arms and the paracord foot strap around it. With your body weight pressing down against the cordage, the paracord will act as an anchor point to help hold your position on the tree. The trick here is to use your leg strength to push yourself up the tree as your arms are merely holding your position as you progress. To get back down to the ground, simply reverse the method you used to climb up. I would not recommend using this strand again, as the abrasive nature of tree bark will take its toll on the integrity of the paracord.

## PROJECT
# SNOW SHOVEL

Snow is a good insulator and can provide a break from the weather by digging a small shelter into it. However, digging down into snow with your hands can be laborious and dangerous if you don't have the right kind of gloves on. Taking a few minutes to make a simple shovel can save a lot of time and prevent your hands from getting frostbitten.

### WHAT YOU WILL NEED

- Tree branch
- Many smaller sticks
- Paracord
- Cutting tool

### Estimated Time for Project

- 15 minutes

**1.** Find a branch that is forked (has a Y shape) on one end and is relatively straight. The Y end of the branch is going to be the shovel end.

**2.** Cut notches along the outsides of the Y pieces. Tie pieces of paracord across the Y section, using the notches to keep them in place.

**3.** Thread paracord through these pieces in an over-under fashion, tying the ends to one another. You can also use cloth, tarp, or wide leaves to add flatness to the shovel.

**4.** On the handle end of the shovel, I like to carve the wood into a blunt spear shape. By flipping the shovel around, I can use the spear end to help break up compacted snow and light ice layers and then haul it away with the shovel end.

The rules for making shelter change when the snow starts falling. Be prepared!

# PROJECT
# SNOWSHOES

Walking through waist-deep snow is slow going and absolutely exhausting. To get around this, you need to spread your weight out over a larger area. The more spread out the weight is, the less you will sink down into the snow. This is why snowshoes are so effective for saving energy and increasing speed when traveling across snow.

The snowshoe frame is easier to make if the piece of wood being used is green, because that makes it more pliable. The frame of the shoe needs to be several times larger than your boot in order to spread out your weight, but if you make it too large then it will be difficult to lift and walk. If you don't take your time to gently bend the branch into shape, it will snap and you will have to start over.

## WHAT YOU WILL NEED

- Branches for the frame and support
- Paracord
- Knife

### Estimated Time for Project

- 1–2 hours

1. Bend the frame into a teardrop shape, then tie the ends together with paracord.

2. Now you need to lay some supports across the middle of it. Pay particular attention to the middle of the shoe where your boot will be placed, because these pieces need to be the strongest in order to support your weight.

3. Place these supports on the bottom of the shoe. A thick piece of wood where the front and back of your boot can rest should be enough.

4. Lay additional small branches across the frame and use paracord to secure it all together.

It's nice to have good snowshoes, but if they aren't in your bug-out bag (see page 22), at least now you know how to make your own rustic version.

**5.** By placing your boot where you want it on the snowshoe, you can use paracord to create a loop or strap that will go across the toe section of your boot. Your boot can be slipped into this strap so that when you lift your foot, the snowshoe comes with it.

**6.** The last step is optional but highly recommended. I like to take whatever vegetation is available (pine boughs are great) and weave it through all of the shoe supports. Doing this prevents snow from pushing up and through the shoe, which will allow you walk higher up on the snow.

### PARA-TIP: Improvise Crampons

In a winter storm, you may find yourself in a slippery situation that can make survival more difficult. You can wrap and tie paracord to the bottoms of your shoes. This will provide enough traction for you to walk across ice with confidence. Tie a couple of overhand knots in the paracord to give a little more gripping power.

## PROJECT
# PULLEY

There are few instances where having a pulley setup can make life less strenuous, such as when you are hoisting gear and food up or moving an obstacle out of your way. I have yet to meet anyone who pulls a pulley out of a pack. This is one reason I like to use heavy-duty shackles for my bracelet closure, because they can be used as an improvised pulley. It will not work exactly the same as a pulley that's made for the job, but it will work.

### WHAT YOU WILL NEED

- **Piece of hardware to use as the pulley center**
- **Paracord**

#### Estimated Time for Project

- **5 minutes**

1. Tie one end of the shackle to a piece of paracord and tie the paracord to a solid anchor point. I tend to use the flat or screw side of the shackle as the anchor point because this leaves the rounded end to be used as the pulley, which works better.

2. Thread a length of paracord through the shackle and tie it off to the object you want to move. By combining the paracord and the shackle, the object should be much easier and quicker to move or lift. If you are planning on staying in one location for an extended amount of time, it might be worthwhile to set one of these up to keep supplies in a safe spot.

## PROJECT
# CROSSING A FROZEN BODY OF WATER

### WHAT YOU WILL NEED

- A large stick or branch
- Paracord

#### Estimated Time for Project

- A few minutes to tie the cord to the branch

Few experiences are as scary as crossing a frozen body of water. Determining whether or not to cross frozen water can greatly impact your travels, depending on how big the body of water is. Trying to find a way around a river or lake could cost days when that time may not be available.

Search the area for a large branch that can be tied to a length of paracord and dragged behind you. You don't want the branch to be so large that it is difficult to pull, but it should be at least twice as long as you are tall. If you break through the ice, you can quickly pull the branch toward you and use it as an anchor across the ice in order to pull yourself up and out.

Count your blessings if there's a bridge! Otherwise, it's either spend hours or days going around, or risking falling in by going straight across. If you have paracord, however, you can give yourself peace of mind.

In a survival situation, the things you carry are precious and must be kept safe. A pack is invaluable because it keeps our supplies organized and easily transportable. However, when a pack gets lost or damaged beyond repair, or you simply didn't have one in the first place, you should be able to adapt.

## HUDSON BAY PACK

No matter your circumstances, you can make a Hudson Bay pack from only a few materials. This style is comfortable to wear and doesn't take much time to make.

**1.** The material for the pack can be anything that you find: a towel, coat, tarp, etc. The best material to use would be something waterproof, but beggars cannot be choosers. Lay out the material that will be used for the pack: in this example, an extra T-shirt.

**2.** Place the items and supplies onto the T-shirt so that they can be rolled up with overlapping sides.

**3.** Twist the ends in the opposite direction in which the pack was rolled, then tie the ends of the shirt into an overhand knot.

**4.** Tie a length of paracord to the knots. The paracord should be long enough that it can be slung over the shoulders and the pack can be carried.

## HOBO PACK

The hobo pack is one of those ways of carrying a small amount of items that might otherwise be annoying to try and fit in your pockets. Traditionally it was composed of a stick, a bandanna, and the items contained in the bandanna. By using paracord to tie the bandanna or other material to the branch, you can carry more things.

**1.** Simply place the items you wish to carry in the middle of a piece of fabric like a bandanna and bring all of the corners up to create a pouch.

**2.** Use paracord to tie the pouch ends to a branch. The branch can easily be carried over your shoulder.

# Collecting Water

Finding a water source can be difficult, but collecting that water can be just as difficult. It is not always going to be as easy as dipping your canteen into a lake or stream. Paracord can make collecting water easier.

**PROJECT: UNREACHABLE WATER (PAGE 208)**

**PROJECT: WATER FILTER (PAGE 209)**

## DRIP LINES

A drip line is extraordinarily helpful if you come upon a water source like a natural spring. Sometimes water will seep out from rock walls and other structures, but because of the low flow rate you can't use the canteen to catch the water. Enter the drip line!

**1.** It may be easier to use one of the inner yarns for this method. Take one end of the yarn and try to place it in a crack or depression underneath where the water is running.

**2.** Pull the yarn slightly away from the wall and place the other end into your canteen. After a bit, the water will begin to run down the line and into the canteen.

This method can also be used if it is raining. It can sometimes be difficult to funnel water into the small openings of water containers. If you see a tree branch where the water is running down steadily, tie a length of paracord to it and place the other end of the cord into a water container. When the water on the branch runs into the paracord, it will be redirected down the cord and into the water container.

## SPONGE METHOD

Just like a cotton T-shirt, a handful of paracord can retain some water for long enough to be squeezed out. A good time to use the sponge method is very early in the day when there is morning dew on all of the vegetation. This method won't produce a lot of water, but when it comes to survival, every drop matters.

**1.** Before the water dries up, use paracord to try and suck up as much of the water as possible.

**2.** When the paracord becomes saturated, squeeze it out into a water container.

# PROJECT
# UNREACHABLE WATER

There may come a time in a survival situation when you find a water source but for some reason can't reach it. Maybe you can't make your way to the source because you are injured, or the water is sitting in the bottom of a deep hole, or maybe it's across a ravine. Whatever the reason, there may be water right in front of you that you can't physically get to. If you have a water container and a long enough length of paracord, you may be able to bring that water to you.

## WHAT YOU WILL NEED

- A water container
- Length of paracord

### Estimated Time for Project

- A few minutes to tie the cord to the container

**1.** Tie one end of the paracord to the container. It must be tied very securely.

**2.** Wrap the other end of the paracord around your hand so the paracord does not get away from you.

**3.** Now comes the fun part. If the water source is below you, lower the container to it. If the water is across a small ravine, chuck the container over the ravine to it.

**4.** Allow the container to sink and fill up. Begin the retrieval process by reeling the paracord back toward you.

With a watertight container and enough paracord, even tricky water becomes accessible.

# PROJECT
# WATER FILTER

Paracord makes a pretty good medium to use for filtering water. Be patient when filtering water this way—it is collected drop by drop. After collecting water from a filter like this, you should still boil it to be safe. You can also reuse the paracord.

**1.** Using a knife, cut the bottom section out of the plastic bottle. This will be the top of the filter where the dirty water is poured through.

**2.** Take as much paracord as you can spare, and make a base layer by compressing it down into the neck of the bottle. Use a stick or tool handle to press the cordage down into the bottle. The tiny pores in paracord will allow water through while trapping the larger debris. On top of that, begin packing any other natural materials that you can find, from smallest to largest: sand, then small rocks, and then larger rocks.

**3.** Once you have all of this in place, set the bottle up where it can stand upright on its own. One easy way to do this is to use paracord to hang the bottle from something.

**4.** Place the collecting container under the water filter. Slowly pour the dirty water in the top of the filter, taking care not to spill water over the edges of the bottle. When the dirty water is poured into the top, large debris like sticks or grass should be filtered out first, and finer material will settle and be filtered out as the water moves down the bottle. The more compacted the layers are, the better the filter will work.

## WHAT YOU WILL NEED

- Plastic bottle or similar container
- Collecting container
- Natural materials, rocks, sand, dirt
- Paracord
- Knife

### Estimated Time for Project

- **15 minutes to make filter, longer to filter dirty water**

# 9 NAVIGATION AND RESCUE

In a survival situation, two options must be evaluated almost daily: should you stay put, or should you attempt to rescue yourself? In situations where a mode of transportation has crashed or broken down, the advice is generally to stay put. That is because the structures (plane, boat, car) can be highly visible, offer protection from the elements, are typically near a traveled path, and have materials that can be scavenged for other uses.

However, a point may come when you realize help is not coming, or you believe you're close enough to civilization to risk traveling. Your best chance of survival may be self-rescue. Paracord can help in navigating your way to safety.

Once you decide to move on, use signaling and navigation techniques to make your plan successful.

# PROJECT
# COMPASS

One of my favorite ways of creating a compass is by magnetizing a needle. A needle is rubbed several times across a piece of silk or a magnet in one direction in order to magnetize it. The needle is then placed onto a small leaf, and the leaf is placed on top of a small body of water that has zero movement in it. The leaf will float on the surface of the water and, because the needle is magnetized, the needle will turn the leaf until the needle is lined up in a north-south direction.

However, even though water covers a vast majority of our planet, you can certainly find yourself in areas where water is in short supply, if there is any at all. Being in such an area, you would think that the above compass couldn't be made, but if you tweak it a bit and use paracord, you're still in luck.

The critical item here is to get the smallest strand from a paracord yarn that you can work with. Tie one end of the yarn to a stable point above the ground so the yarn hangs down. Tie the other end around the middle section of a needle and magnetize the needle. Carefully let the needle go so that it hangs as horizontally as possible in the air. The very thin yarn should allow the needle to spin and reach a north-south orientation.

## WHAT YOU WILL NEED

- Paracord yarns
- Needle or other small piece of metal that can be magnetized
- Silk or a magnet

### Estimated Time for Project

- 5 minutes

As can you see in the picture, I tore the inner yarn apart until it was just fine fibers. This allows the needle to spin under less tension. Be patient, as placing the yarn directly in the middle of the needle is quite the balancing act.

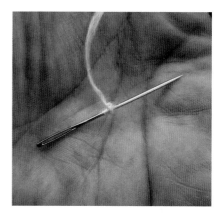

# PROJECT
# DRAFTING COMPASS

A drafting compass may seem a bit rudimentary, but it can be helpful in calculating distances. Along with a map, you should always carry a writing utensil and some paper in your pack. For the writing utensils, I personally like to carry a permanent marker, some type of pen, and several wood pencils.

Take your pencil and tie a piece of paracord around the end of it. The end of the paracord can be placed in a desired position and held in place. The rest of the cord is held taut, and lines or arcs can be drawn. Use one hand to hold down the paracord end while using the other hand to make marks with the writing utensil. Most maps also have a scale that helps in converting distances. A piece of the paracord can be lined up with the scale and used to determine distance on the map.

If you don't have something to write with, a little ingenuity will allow you to still use this method. Find a small piece of wood that can be sharpened at one end to look like a pencil. Char the sharpened end over a fire, but don't let the wood burn all of the way through. The blackened layer of the wood will now act like a pencil.

## WHAT YOU WILL NEED

- Writing utensil
- Length of paracord
- Map
- Paper

### Estimated Time for Project

- A few minutes

## PROJECT
# TRAIL BLAZING

Whenever I think of trail blazing, I think of Hansel and Gretel and the breadcrumbs they used to find their way out of the woods. It can be easy to get turned around in certain environments, or you may hit a point where you have to backtrack. When this happens, trail blazing will help in finding your way back and indicating if you have accidentally circled around.

Cut the paracord into roughly 6 in. (15 cm) lengths. If you have the paracord to spare, you can make them longer to increase visibility, as shown in the photo. As you are walking, periodically tie one of these lengths to a tree branch or hang it from something else. It's best to tie the markers on the side of the tree in the direction that you are walking. When you look back, you will see the paracord markers in proper orientation.

## WHAT YOU WILL NEED

- Several 6 in. (15 cm) lengths of paracord
- Cutting tool

### Estimated Time for Project

- A couple minutes per blaze

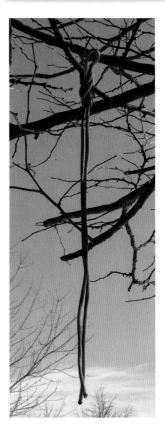

When it comes to trail blazing, the more your paracord stands out, the better.

# PROJECT
# DRAG LINES

It's easy to become disoriented walking in very thick vegetation, as I found out in the rainforests of Ecuador. Even walking only a few hundred feet away from camp, I never felt more lost in my life. There was so much plant life that it was difficult to distinguish physical markers of any kind. It was there that I found a great way to keep track of my movements.

By tying a length of paracord to your pack and letting it drag along the ground behind you as you walk, you create a trail behind you. Every so often, stop and look back at your drag line. If the line is straight, then your path is true. If it bends and turns, then you can still see where you have come from.

## WHAT YOU WILL NEED

- **Long lengths of paracord**

### Estimated Time for Project

- **A few minutes**

In a seemingly endless forest, leaving a trail can be invaluable.

# MAKING PACE COUNT BEADS

Pace count beads, or ranger beads, are a means of estimating distance while you are walking. The only downside to this tool is that you need to have an accurate assessment of how many paces you take in a certain distance.

Use a tape measure to mark off a 100 meter path, or use a running track. Count how many paces it takes to walk this path. Repeat this process several times and average your paces. You now know how many paces it takes you to travel 100 meters.

Pace count beads may look a little confusing at first, but they are easy to understand. Hang the pace count beads in an accessible place, such as on the straps of your pack. Make sure all of the beads are pushed to the top of their section. The bottom beads are going to be your pace counters, and the top beads are going to represent the distance walked.

After you have walked and counted your paces to reach 100 meters, slide one of the bottom beads all of the way down. After every 100 meters walked, slide another bottom bead down. The last bead to be pushed down will represent 900 meters walked and there will be no more beads in the bottom section to slide. Walk another 100 meters and slide down one of the top beads and reset the bottom beads by pushing them all back up. You have now

covered a distance of 1,000 meters, which is represented by one of the top beads being pushed down. Continue this process by counting off the 100 meter distance and sliding down the bottom beads.

To make this project, use a small length of paracord and standard arts and craft beads. A hobby store may be hard to come by in a survival situation, so I will also show another material you can use instead of beads (see page 218).

**1.** First make the frame for the beads to slide onto. The frame is made up of two sections: upper and lower. The lower section needs to be larger than the upper section because it will hold more beads. A simple overhand knot can be used on both ends of the cord and in the middle to separate the two sections. Fold the paracord in half to find the midsection and tie an overhand knot using both of the cords. Leave a loop at the top so that the finished project can easily be attached to a pack strap.

**2.** Begin sliding the beads onto the paracord. The upper section will contain four beads while the lower section contains nine beads. To make this easier, burn the cut ends of the paracord and twist them in between your fingers so that they are thin and pointed. Thread both ends of the cord through the beads and slide four beads all the way to the top knot. Leave at least 1 in. (2.5 cm) between the last bead and the second overhand knot so that they have room to slide down. I decided to add a bit of style this time: I am using beads that are shaped like skulls, with glow-in-the-dark eyes.

By tying a few simple overhand knots around the frame, you can create improvised beads. You can also use pieces of wood for the beads. Cut thirteen small pieces of wood approximately 1 in. (2.5 cm) long. Using the tip of your knife, drill a hole through the wood so that the paracord can be threaded through. After all of the wood beads are ready, use the steps in the first method of the project to build the pace count beads.

**3.** Thread the last nine beads onto the paracord and slide them up to the second overhand knot. Again, leave at least 1 in. (2.5 cm) of space after the last bead and tie an overhand knot.

**4.** You can get by with a single overhand knot. Leave the "arms" on either side of the knot, because every so often the knots need to be tightened.

# Signaling

As you are navigating your way to safety and getting closer to civilization, there will be an increased chance of encountering people who could help you. When the possibility of rescue presents itself, you need to do everything possible to be seen. Color, sound, movement, and light are all things to keep in mind when trying to signal.

**PROJECT: BRIGHT COLORS (PAGE 220)**

**PROJECT: FIRE AND SMOKE (PAGE 221)**

**PROJECT: KITE (PAGE 222)**

## PROJECT
# BRIGHT COLORS

My trusty shammy works great as a flag.

### WHAT YOU WILL NEED

- Brightly colored paracord
- Article of clothing

#### Estimated Time for Project

- A few minutes

Brightly colored paracord (orange or pink) is going to be much easier to see from a distance than something that will blend into the natural surroundings. When the opportunity arises to be rescued, tie a brightly colored article of clothing to the end of a length of paracord and swing it around in a large circle while yelling or using a signaling whistle. Alternatively, tie a piece of material to a branch. This way, if you are completing other tasks, or sleeping, there will always be something visible for others to see. This is especially effective on windy days.

### PARA-TIP: Defy Nature with Straight Lines

I once heard a saying that goes something like, "God does not create things in straight lines." Almost everything naturally created is not exactly straight. You can use this to your advantage when signaling for help. Paracord is fairly straight on its own, so hanging or laying out several lengths of it where it can easily be seen from a distance will draw the attention of search parties. Use contrasting colors between the paracord and natural surroundings for best results.

# PROJECT
# FIRE AND SMOKE

A signal fire can be a great way of getting the attention of a search party. But how can paracord help with a signal fire, you may ask? On pages 143 through 151, I describe a number of ways in which paracord can help with starting a fire, which you will need for a signal fire.

There are two aspects of a fire that you should think about when using it specifically for signaling: the size of the fire and the smoke that is produced. Depending on its location, a fire that produces little to no smoke can still be seen from a long way off, especially at night.

To make a signal fire even more visible, construct a tripod with a raised platform where the fire can be placed. Be sure to place a layer of sand or dirt beneath the fire so that it doesn't burn through the platform. Obviously the bigger you make the fire, the more visible it will be, but keep a few things in mind. Don't make a fire so big you can't control it, and always pay attention to your surroundings. Making a big fire in the middle of a dry prairie or forest on a windy day is a terrible idea!

To make a column of thick white smoke, put green vegetation onto the base of an established fire. This white column will be seen best on sunny, cloudless days. When possible, make a signal fire in a place where there is open sky above it, instead of under a tree canopy. While smoke can get through tree canopies, it will become diffused.

**PARA-TIP: Don't Burn Your Paracord Supply**

When paracord is burned, it will produce unhealthy black smoke, which can also be highly visible. Not recommended! First, it would take a lot of paracord to produce enough black smoke to be seen. Secondly, even if you have enough paracord to accomplish this, there is a chance you still might not be seen. In that scenario, you are not being rescued and you have sacrificed all of your paracord.

# PROJECT
## KITE

Kites can take the form of many different shapes, sizes, and designs, but for simplicity, a simple cross-shaped kite is your best bet.

You can get a kite high in the air, *very high*. The end goal of any survival situation is being rescued, and having a kite hovering 100 ft. (30 m) up in the air is going to increase your chances of being seen.

## WHAT YOU WILL NEED

- **Lots of paracord yarns**
- **A piece of light but strong material**
- **2 lightweight, strong sticks**

### Estimated Time for Project

- **30 minutes**

1. Find two sticks where one of them is at least several times longer than the other. These sticks need to be as light as possible but also strong. Tie the two sticks together in the shape of a cross. The next step involves finding some lightweight material that will catch the wind. One of the items I always carry in my pack is a large, heavy-duty trash bag, because they serve a multitude of purposes. Substitute any suitable material you can find.

2. Once you have found kite-flying material, lay it over the frame and tie it tightly to the four points of the frame using pieces of yarn. The end of the long yarn should be secured to the midsection of the cross frame. The rest of the yarn should be wrapped around a small piece of wood so that you don't accidentally lose the kite during flight.

PROJECT
# RAFT AND PADDLE

One of the oldest and probably best-known pieces of survival advice is to follow water sources downhill or downstream. By following a stream or river, you should increase your chances of finding help. A water source can also speed your travels along if a raft can be constructed. For this project, I am not listing specific materials needed for the raft because those can vary depending on the environment you find yourself in. Generally, lengths of some material, tree branches, logs, bamboo, and so forth will need to be lashed together, and paracord is certainly strong enough to get the job done.

You will definitely also want an oar or a paddle. This will help in propelling the raft, steering, and slowing down. No matter which of the types of paddle you decide to make, I highly recommend that a length of paracord be tied from the handle to the raft or boat. A paddle can be easily dropped and lost in the water, leaving you literally up a creek without a paddle.

## WHAT YOU WILL NEED
- **Material for the raft**
- **Paracord**

### Estimated Time for Project
- **Depends on the raft material available**

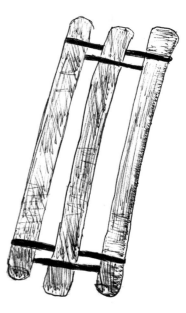

Use an over-under method of wrapping the paracord around a series of logs to lash them together. Make sure to tightly cinch the lashings to securely hold the logs in place.

**Option 1.** Making an improvised paddle is going to be very similar to the snow shovel project (see page 200). Use a branch that has a Y shape in it at one end and as straight as possible. A branch with a deep curve or bend in it is going to be harder and less efficient to use in the water. Stretch a piece of material (waterproof bag, a piece of a tarp, etc.) over the Y section and secure it tightly with paracord. Just like that, you have a paddle for your craft.

**Option 2.** If you have an ax or knife, split a large branch or log to produce a flat surface that will be the paddle. Place this flat on the ground with the branch handle lying on top of it. Position the branch so that it is in the middle of the paddle. On both sides of the branch, make two marks that will need to be "drilled" through. There should be at least three pairs of theses holes in order to secure the branch. Thread paracord through the holes and around the branch and tie it all together. It may help to cut shallow notches in the branch handle where the paracord will wrap around. This will hold the branch tighter to the paddle and keep it from slipping up and down.

The above oar consists of a long branch and piece of wood with notches cut in both pieces. By cutting small, even notches in the wood, the paracord will hold the two pieces together much better.

### PARA-TIP: Coconut Flotation Devices

If you find yourself on an island or shore with coconuts, you can actually use them for this purpose. Whole coconuts are impervious to water and contain air so they naturally float. By lashing many of them together, you can make a floater to hold onto while in the water.

**Option 3.** Find a branch or log that is thick enough in diameter that a paddle can be carved from one piece.

The more time you spend making your raft water-ready, the better off you'll be when the going gets rough!

## PARA-TIP: Parachute-Style Flotation Devices

Find material that is as nonporous as possible: parachute, trash bags, and some types of clothing. Grab a section of this material with both hands and swing it around in order to fill it with air. When enough air has been collected, bring the ends together as quickly as possible and tie it shut in order to trap the air inside. You most likely will not be able to make this container airtight. Only use this type of floater for short crossings lest you find yourself doggy paddling the rest of the way.

## PARA-TIP: Plastic Bottle Flotation Devices

An unfortunate side effect of humans living on the planet is the amount of trash we produce and how we dispose of it. It's lucky for the survivor that this trash has a way of being carried to almost every corner in the world. Probably the most common type of trash that a person can find in the wild is plastic, especially plastic bottles. If you come upon a trove of plastic bottles, they can be lashed together much like coconuts (see page 224) and be used to float across the water.

# PROJECT
# DEPTH GAUGE

When trying to walk out of some environments, you may come to a waterway or waterfall that seems impassable. Time can be crucial in survival situations, so a choice will need to be made: do you jump in so that you can continue, or do you look for a way around?

If you choose to jump, you need to consider both the height of the jump and the depth of the water you are jumping into. For this second consideration, if you have paracord and a rock, you can get a pretty accurate estimate of the depth.

## WHAT YOU WILL NEED

- **Long length of paracord**
- **Rock**

**Estimated Time for Project**

- **20 minutes**

**1.** Pick a rock. Your rock must be heavy enough that it will sink right away and not be affected by the current of the water.

**2.** Tie one end of the paracord around the rock, crisscrossing the paracord around the rock. Make sure the rock will not fall out of the paracord.

**3.** Throw the rock into the water that you plan to jump in. If the water is accompanied by a waterfall, the area you plan to jump in should be beyond the whitewater of the falls. This is because the whitewater is full of air bubbles, and if you jump into this, you will sink much faster and farther into the water, possibly hitting the bottom.

**4.** Once the rock has hit the bottom, begin pulling it up and measuring the cordage at the same time. For me, I know that when my arms are stretched out side to side, the distance from fingertip to fingertip is roughly 5 ft. (1.5 m). Keep track of the measurements until the rock breaks the water's surface.

### PARA-TIP: Beat the Fog with Paracord

When there are several people walking together in the wild, there is always a chance of losing a group member because they wandered off or lost sight of the other members. This can easily happen if visibility is low due to fog, rain, snow, or heavy vegetation. An easy way to make sure all of the group members stick together is by linking everyone together with lengths of paracord.

# 10 OUTSIDE-THE-BOX PARACORD USES

Paracord has a lot of uses that may not be immediately obvious—filling up free time included!

# Miscellaneous Paracord Uses

The following are some extra ideas on how you can use paracord that don't require much explanation.

- Use as suspenders to keep your pants up
- Use as a simple belt
- Tighten loose areas of clothes to keep the cold out: sleeves, pant legs
- Keep long hair out of your face by using it to make a ponytail
- Tie items to your pack for easy carrying
- Tie the bottom of your pants shut to prevent creepy crawlers from finding their way up your leg
- Replace webbing on a pack
- Replace a broken line on a boat anchor
- Use the yarns as dental floss
- Tie a boat to shore
- If you have a pull-start boat motor, it can be used as a replacement pull-start cord

- Make a fish stringer for keeping fish alive in the water. When using this, I suggest pushing the line through the bottom of the fish's mouth and not through the gills.
- Use as a vehicle towline. Make as many passes as you can between the two vehicles with the paracord. This will make the improvised towline stronger. Or you can use the ropes that you made earlier in the book.
- Lower or raise gear over steep embankments so that you can more safely climb them
- Hang up a lantern or flashlight at camp
- Use as a clothesline

- **Make sure you never lose your glasses by making a simple lanyard**

Eye protection is always important, so if you have them, keep them handy with a paracord lanyard. By using brightly colored paracord, they will be easy to spot if they accidentally fall into the brush.

- Keep loose items organized by tying them together
- Tie up pets so they don't wander off at night
- If you are traveling by horseback, paracord can be used in a number of ways to fix harnesses, attach items to the saddle, and use as a lead
- Fix or make a dog collar or leash
- Affix an arrowhead to an arrow shaft
- Tie feathers to an arrow shaft for fletchings
- Clean firearm barrels
- Tie a few overhand knots in a length and pull it through water bag straws in order to help clean them
- Use it to play cat's cradle or other string games in order to entertain kids or yourself
- Use as a bush washcloth for cleaning purposes

- **A pile of fluffed-out yarn makes for a good collector when making wood shavings for fire starting**

- Anchor writing tools to the inside of a pocket or a notebook with a paracord yarn
- Make a harness for pulling a sled
- Make a simple tree swing for a place to sit and relax
- Set up a zipline to move materials from one place to another (*not* for moving people)
- If you have a bow and arrow at your disposal, tie one end of paracord or a yarn to an arrow in order to shoot cordage over a tree branch or across a gorge to another team member. This could also be used as a means of bow fishing.
- Make a lanyard for carrying mementos you may find along your journey

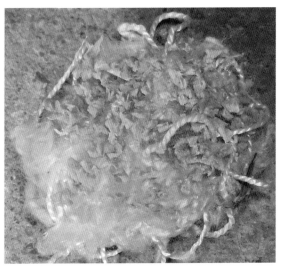

A fluffed-up yarn ball mixed with fatwood shavings makes for a great fire starter.

- Use a length of paracord as a lifeline when swimming in water by tying one end to a boat or an anchor point on shore and holding the other end
- Make a jump rope for staying in shape or to cure boredom
- Hoist and hold animals in the air in order to skin them easier
- Use as safety tie-offs while using proper climbing gear
- Sew hides together for clothing or bags

- Leave a trail of those paracord scraps you have in your pocket. They might be so small they can't be used for anything else, but they just might catch the eye of a SAR (search and rescue) team.

- **Pair yarn with a coffee filter to make an improvised tea bag for brewing tasty wilderness drinks**

I always carry some coffee filters in my pack because they have a number helpful uses (besides giving me my caffeine fix). If you know your plants, this is a good way of making a warm brew of wild tea.

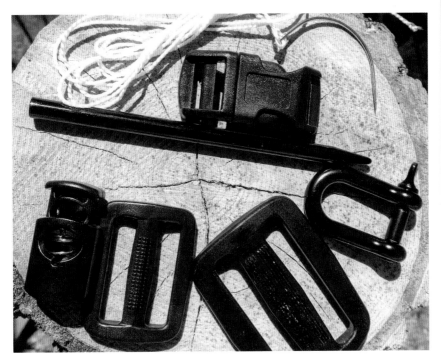

Items I like to carry in my pack for gear repair. (Pictured top to bottom: curved sewing needle and yarns, plastic buckle, paracord threading needle, metal shackle, two different sizes of sliding buckles, a toggle.)

# Gear Repair

In a survival situation, what you have with you is all that you have until you find your way to safety. Those items you wore are now worth their weight in gold. But due to circumstances or time, gear will break down. It should never be discarded unless absolutely necessary.

Most gear repair work involves fixing holes in your pack or other fabrics. Deciding to use a whole piece of yarn or a pulled-apart piece for sewing depends on how much paracord you have, the size of the repair, and the desired strength. For example, footwear is very important, and shoes take a lot of abuse. When repairing shoes or boots, use a whole piece of yarn. However, if you are fixing a small hole in your shirt, pull the yarn apart and use a smaller piece.

# REPAIRING A DRAWSTRING POUCH

I like to carry a drawstring bag in my pack because they are very versatile. I especially like a mesh bag: wet items, like clothes, can be carried in them while still drying a bit. A needle is not required to repair this, but it sure does make the repair much easier. Use a whole piece of paracord.

First, install the threading needle to one end of the cord. Next, weave the needle in and out of the mesh holes all of the way around the top of the bag. Make sure you have enough paracord so that you don't pull one end through the starting point. Next, use a toggle.

A toggle will help keep items from falling out by keeping the pouch closed. The ends of the paracord should be burned and rolled into a point to get them through the toggle hole. Once both of the ends are through, tie a simple overhand knot to prevent the toggle from sliding off. If there is more paracord than desired after the knot, cut off the excess and burn the ends.

## WHAT YOU WILL NEED

- Paracord
- **Cutting tool**
- **Lighter**
- **Toggle**
- **Needle (optional but is a big help)**

### Estimated Time for Project

- **10 minutes**

PROJECT

# REPAIRING PACK STRAPS

A pack with broken carrying straps is pretty inconvenient. As long as there are two points to secure a piece of paracord to, straps can be improvised very easily. If the straps are uncomfortable, additional padding can be added by any means possible.

## WHAT YOU WILL NEED

- A length of paracord
- Cutting tool

### Estimated Time for Project

- 10 minutes

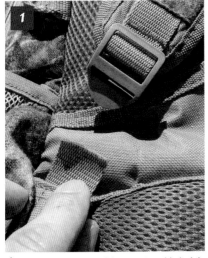

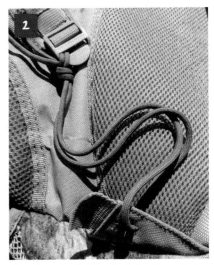

**1.** The upper portion of the strap is padded while the bottom is connected to nylon webbing via a plastic buckle. The webbing and the buckle are what make the strap adjustable. Over time, the nylon wore out, became frayed, and eventually fell apart.

**2.** I'm lucky that the plastic buckle on the top strap is still intact, because it gives me at least one anchor point for tying the paracord. I took a length of paracord and threaded one end through the slide buckle. Using my knife, I cut a small hole in the material of the bottom strap and threaded the end of the paracord through that. I then looped the cord back up, passed it through the buckle, and tied both ends in an overhand knot.

## FIXING A ZIPPER HANDLE

Depending on the size of the zipper base, a yarn or a piece of whole paracord can be used. A hollowed-out outer sheath can also be used. It helps to use a lighter to melt and roll the end of the paracord into a fine point. Thread the melted end through the hole in the zipper base and tie it off. A braid can be made around this initial core to make a small handle. As usual, my go-to braid is the cobra weave.

The pictured zipper pull is a simple one because I didn't have the time to make a handle. I used a hollowed scrap of paracord that I threaded through the zipper. At the midpoint of the cord, I tied a couple of overhand knots so that the zipper pull wouldn't slip back and forth when I used it. I then joined the cut ends using a fisherman's knot.

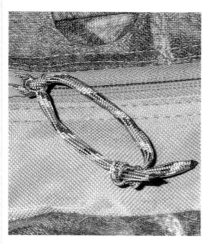

## FIXING A BUTTON

Buttons and toggles are easy to make from wood and are quite useful. A wood button and toggle can be made in less than twenty minutes, especially if a wood saw is available. For a button, I use the tip of my knife to drill a small hole in the center of a small piece of wood.

Toggles are even easier; a small piece of wood with a shallow groove cut all the way around the center will work as an improvised toggle. For both hardware pieces, a single yarn is sufficient to anchor them onto gear items, unless of course you make them bigger than normal.

# REPAIRING SHOES AND BOOTS

When it comes to footwear, there is always one thing that I do first when I get a new pair of outdoor shoes or boots: replace the laces with paracord. There are two reasons that I do this. The first is that it is a handy way to carry some extra cordage while still being functional. The second is that the paracord laces tend to hold up better and longer than the original laces.

There have been a few times when I have torn a hole in my footwear or some of the material has separated. If you have a strong needle, or makeshift awl, you can temporarily fix this damage by sewing the material back together with the inner yarns from a length of paracord.

## WHAT YOU WILL NEED

- Paracord and paracord yarns
- Needle or makeshift awl in order to make holes

### Estimated Time for Project

- 20 minutes

The laces on this boot are almost 5 ft. (1.5 m) long. That gives a total of roughly 80 ft. (24 m) of paracord when used for both boots.

I was able to fix a hole in the side of my tennis shoes with a short yarn, a large curved needle, and about ten minutes of work.

## PROJECT
# SEWING HOLES

A hole in a pack can be devastating and should be addressed as soon as possible. As long you have inner yarns from a length of paracord, you can sew until the cows come home.

## WHAT YOU WILL NEED

- Needle or makeshift awl to make holes
- Paracord yarns

### Estimated Time for Project

- Depends on the size of the repair

**1.** Here I had a hole that wasn't too large, but it was right under the top carrying strap, so it wouldn't take much for it to get worse. Thread a yarn through the needle's eye. Use a larger needle and a whole yarn piece, because a pack has to carry a good deal of weight. After threading the needle, double the yarn over so that you are sewing with two pieces of material. When you first push the needle through both pieces of material, make a few knots—you pick which ones—to close up one of the ends.

**2.** As you can see, I am using a rather large needle. I believe this one came in a pack of different upholstery needles. If you are having trouble finding similar needles, visit your local fabric store.

**3.**

**3.** Push the needle through the material, pull the yarn tight, go up and over the material, and push the needle through again. Basically, make a continuous line of loops (similar to the running stitch) along the patch. Sew under and around the carrying strap. By incorporating the strap, the patch should be stronger.

Here I am using a much smaller needle to fix my shirt. Once a hole begins in a piece of fabric, it will only get worse unless it's taken care of. The outdoors can be hard on clothes, and you don't want to find your jeans turned into jean shorts, or your shirt into a crop top. In the photos above and below, I am taking care of both of those articles of clothing by using paracord yarns (pulled apart) and a needle.

Sooner or later I always get holes in the knee section of my jeans. A broken-down piece of yarn, a needle, and about ten minutes, and the jeans are ready to go again.

## QUICK PARA-HACKS

### REPAIRING A WATCHBAND

A broken watchband can have you wondering where to keep your watch safe. You can use the cobra weave braid (see page 70 for instructions) to make a new watchband. A paracord watchband doesn't really give a lot of cordage, so keep in mind that this is strictly a gear fix.

### PARACORD GLUE

Melted paracord adheres quite well to other nylon products and even temporarily to other synthetic materials. This works best for minor repairs, since it can take a lot of paracord to produce enough glue. By using a fire source, the end of a piece of paracord can be lit and heated until a glob of melted nylon forms. The melted glob can then be applied to other material in need of repair. Applying the "glue" should be done as quickly as possible because the melted nylon cools and hardens quickly. I recommend having a small twig or other tool available to help spread the melted material. This will save you from burning your fingertips.

# GLOSSARY

**550 CORD:** Paracord with seven to nine inner yarns that can hold 550 pounds (250 kilograms) of static weight. Its full name is type III 550 cord.

**EZ SPLICER:** Tool that aids in pulling paracord through tight spaces.

**FATWOOD:** Wood that is dense in flammable resin.

**FERROCERIUM ROD:** A metal rod that produces sparks when scraped against another metal surface. Used for starting a fire.

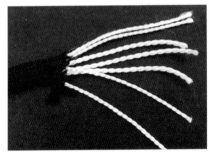

550 CORD

FATWOOD

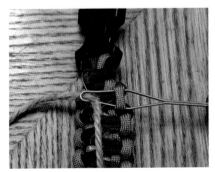

EZ SPLICER

FERROCERIUM ROD

**FUEL:** Wood for fire making that is anything larger than kindling.

**HEMOSTATS:** Resemble small needle-nose pliers that help in pulling paracord through tight spaces. They often can be clamped down on material using the locking handles.

**KINDLING:** Pieces of wood for fire making that should be no thicker than your thumb.

**MAGNESIUM ROD:** A rod that magnesium shavings can be scraped from for starting a fire. Magnesium shavings are combustible and burn extremely hot.

**PARACORD THREADING NEEDLE:** A large, hollow, blunt needle with threads on one end. A paracord end can be threaded into the hollow needle where it is held in place. This helps in projects with lots of weaving in and out of tight spaces.

HEMOSTATS

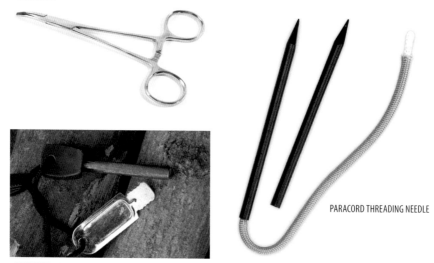

MAGNESIUM ROD

PARACORD THREADING NEEDLE

**SHACKLES:** A type of hardware that is often used as a closure in paracord bracelets and other projects.

**YARNS:** The strands that make up the core of paracord.

**TINDER:** Material used for fire making that should have as much surface area as possible so that it will take a spark easily.

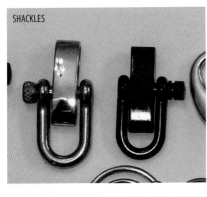

SHACKLES

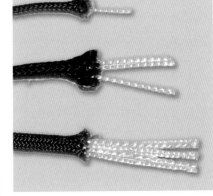

YARNS

TINDER

# ADDITIONAL PARACORD RESOURCES

The purpose of this book was to create a travel-size reference for paracord survival projects. Because there is so much information and different techniques out there, I couldn't possibly fit it all into a single book. So I wanted to share some great resources I have used in learning about paracord in order to help you along your journey.

## Pepperell Braiding Company

*www.pepperell.com*

Offers physical resources like paracord and hardware as well as walk-throughs for completing certain paracord projects.

## Stormdrane

*www.stormdrane.blogspot.com*

This blog has some of the most beautiful and unique paracord projects I have come across and was my original inspiration for braiding projects.

## Gladding Paracord

*www.gladdingbraid.com*

This is some of the best U.S.-made paracord around. I have used their paracord for years, and I have never once been dissatisfied with their product.

The following website does not deal with paracord specifically but is a great resource for further learning about survival and preparedness skills.

## Nature Reliance School

*www.naturereliance.org*

# ABOUT THE AUTHOR

This is Bryan Lynch's second book, following *Victorinox Swiss Army Knife Camping & Outdoor Survival Guide: 101 Tips, Tricks & Uses* (also published by Fox Chapel Publishing). He lives in the American Midwest with his wife and kids.

# ACKNOWLEDGMENTS

When I was younger and picked up a book, the only name I ever thought about was the author. After all, the author wrote it, so who else is there, right? As with the production of many things, there are a lot of people behind the scenes we don't give much thought to. However, without their hard work and dedication, my scribbles on paper couldn't have been turned into the finished book before you. I would like to thank my editor, Bud Sperry, who guided me through the process of the book world and answered so many phone calls and e-mails from me that, looking back, I wonder how in the world he got any other work done. To all of the fine people at Fox Chapel Publishing whose hands shaped my manuscript into a work that I could never imagine, I thank you. I would like to thank Joel Hooks from Pepperell Braiding Company for providing resources that helped in the making of many projects in this book. I can attest to the quality of their paracord and paracord-related products after extensively testing them.

To my friends and family whose teachings through the years added up to the accumulation of knowledge in these pages. A special thank you to a small group of friends, you know who you are, who have supported me from the beginning of my paracord journey when I didn't even know what paracord was. You guys kept me going and tested every little project I threw at you. Thank you to my parents who always encouraged me to spend so much time outdoors where I had to figure things out for myself, a necessity in life. Dad, thank you for showing me that patience, silence, and observation are a lost art in the ways of today but are essential in the natural world. Our parents are our first teachers, and mine gave me more than I could ever repay; I hope you both get to rest now because you deserve it. Joan and Bill, your help and support has not gone unnoticed and, quite frankly, you two are awesome. Above all, I thank my wife, Nikki, because I know a lot of time has been sacrificed so that I could create this work. I value your encouragement, support, opinions, and advice above all others. Also thank you for allowing me to make a complete mess out of our house with research material and projects. Now that the book is complete, I will begin cleaning up my messes.

# INDEX

Note: Page numbers in *italics* indicate projects and hacks. Page numbers in **bold** indicate glossary terms.

# IMAGE CREDITS

All illustrations and photographs by the author except as listed here. The following images are credited to Shutterstock.com and their respective creators: front cover main image: FotoCor78; front cover mountains: Galyna Andrushko; back cover landscape: Yevhenii Chulovskyi; spine: Stock image; para-tip icon on page 13 and throughout: matsabe; page 1: Murzina Elena Sergeevna; page 2: Stock image; pages 6–7: Stock image; page 10 top: Everett Collection; pages 14–15: Stock image; pages 16–17: Diego Cervo; page 17: Mega Pixel; page 20: Aleksandr Bryliaev; page 21 top: M. Arkhipov; page 21 bottom: PSR1980; page 22: ArtStudioHouse; page 23 green cord: PauliusKpm; page 23 gray tarp: endeavor; page 23 compass: Good Luck Photo; page 23 firestarter: Raisman; page 23 map: HomeStudio; page 23 water bottle: Kidsada Manchinda; pages 24–25: Petrychenko Anton; page 25: BonNontawat; page 30 bottom: lmbi photos; page 51 top: Sergey Sharonov; page 52 top: BW Folsom; pages 56–57: Lutsenko_Oleksandr; page 57: FotoCor78; page 68 top: Nor Gal; pages 110–111: Eva Kali; page 112: Paul Winterman; page 114: Background Land; pages 138–139: Benevolente82; page 139: Dmytro Sheremeta; page 140 diagram: seamuss; pages 140–141: bmphotographer; page 145: zlikovec; page 146 top: Bogdan Denysyuk; page 152: Kristen Prahl; pages 154–155: Nicole Glass Photography; page 155: Gunnar Pippel; page 156: Emilija Miljkovic; page 166: optimarc; page 169: Igor Chus; pages 170–171: James Aloysius Mahan V; page 171: James Aloysius Mahan V; page 175: Daniel Requena Lambert; page 176 top: Kimberly Boyles; page 182 top: Vitalii Nesterchuk; page 182 bottom left: mark_gusev; page 182 bottom right: Brent Hofacker; page 183: mark_gusev; page 186: Brent Hofacker; pages 188–189: ESOlex; page 189: prokoole; page 191: Andrey Burmakin; page 200: Robsonphoto; page 202: marekuliasz; page 204: Salvador Maniquiz; page 206 top: Chonlawut; page 206 bottom left: Atosan; page 208: Atosan; pages 210–211: aribic; page 211: Eakachai Leesin; page 215: Vladimir Kurilov; page 219 top: frantic00; page 225: AleksKo; page 227: rui vale sousa; pages 228–229: Erica Marroquin; page 229: Mariusz Szczygiel; page 236 right: antkevyv; page 241 bottom right: jonny neesom; page 242 top left: Paii VeGa; page 242 bottom left: Boris Pralovszky